Praise for David J. Pollay and *The Law of the Garbage Truck*

There's a simple reason why David J. Pollay's "No Garbage Trucks! Pledge" has been translated into 48 languages, and people from more than 100 countries have taken it: It works! Start living a better life now!

—Nick Morgan, President of Public Words, and author of
Trust Me: Four Steps to Authenticity and Charisma

Follow David J. Pollay's powerful recommendations . . . and you'll develop positive habits of happiness.

—Ed Diener, Joseph R. Smiley Distinguished Professor of Psychology, University of Illinois, coauthor
(with Robert Biswas-Diener) of *Happiness: Unlocking the Mysteries of Psychological Wealth*

One of the best books I've read in years . . . you'll want everyone you care about to read *The Law of the Garbage Truck.*

—Yakov Smirnoff, America's Funniest Russian Comedian, and Professor at Missouri State University

As a Yahoo!, David was a one man "No Garbage Zone" of positive attitude and good business results. This honest and generous book will show you how to be one too.

—Tim Sanders, former Chief Solutions Officer at Yahoo!, and author of
Love Is the Killer App: How to Win Business and Influence Friends

This enjoyable, fast-moving book shows you how to forget about past events you cannot change, and focus on creating an unlimited future for yourself.

—Brian Tracy, author, 55 books/38 languages

Athletes committed to greatness need to study *The Law of the Garbage Truck*. Like a great coach, David J. Pollay offers a powerful game plan for success in life and sports.

—Jeff Conine, Major League Baseball All-Star and two-time World Series winner

How you interact with the world is a choice. You can get dumped on (and do some dumping). Or you can enjoy life. It's your decision and David J. Pollay will show you how to make it. —David Meerman Scott, best-selling author of *The New Rules of Marketing & PR*

To know the essence of motivation is to reach in your soul and see how far you can push your heart! In *The Law of the Garbage Truck*, David J. Pollay helps you visit that feeling.

—Ronnie Lott, member of the National Football League Hall of Fame

I'm recommending *The Law of the Garbage Truck* to everyone I know. David J. Pollay gives us what we need—a common language to revolutionize our relationships at home, at work, and in the world. —Scott Dols, CEO of Trucks.com

This book is full of delightfully practical advice on how to focus on the right things to improve our lives and our relationships.

—James O. Pawelski, Director of Education and Senior Scholar,
Positive Psychology Center at the University of Pennsylvania

A MUST READ for business leaders today. I have handed out copies of *The Law of the Garbage Truck* to my colleagues and team members.

—Frank Sui, Partner, Deloitte Consulting LLP

The Law of the Garbage Truck has everything necessary to become a classic in the empowerment field.
—Caroline Adams Miller, author of *Creating Your Best Life: The Ultimate Life List Guide*

Whether you are in business, academia, a parent, spouse, or just getting out of school, this book will change your life forever.
—Alberto B. Casellas, Vice President and General Manager, General Electric Capital Retail Finance

I want every principal, teacher, and parent to read *The Law of the Garbage Truck*. This brilliant book shows us how to give our best to our children every day, and to each other.
—Tammy Ferguson, North Area Director of School Accountability, Palm Beach County School District

Cancer patients long for the time they will be able to move beyond unanswered questions and gripping fears to a feeling of well-being, strength, and focus. *The Law of the Garbage Truck* is a liberating tool.
—Lenora Johnson, Founder and Executive Director,
Steel Magnolias Breast Cancer Support Group, Inc.

The universality of this spiritual message goes beyond all borders and unites all of us in a single mission to be kind and compassionate to all people.
—Reverend Linda Mobley, Cason United Methodist Church of Delray Beach

David J. Pollay pours his naturally infectious positive energy into a clear, pragmatic formula to magnetize your own positive mindset in life and business.
—Rick Brandon, author of *Survival of the Savvy: High-Integrity Political Tactics for Career and Company Success*

Pollay has profound empathy for people's daily struggle to find kindness in the world. If we all chose to live by his simple principles, we would be on our way to achieving peace in our day.
—Michele Trickey, President and CEO of AIESEC in the United States

In reading *The Law of the Garbage Truck*, I was reminded of the teachings of the Dalai Lama. Many of David Pollay's insightful observations and helpful recommendations are rooted in the time honored principles of Buddhism.
—Dale Smith, Head of School, Pine Crest School

David J. Pollay has written a superb and deeply spiritual book. *The Law of the Garbage Truck* instructs us to cleanse our spirits . . . and invites us to pursue a deep introspection in a way that inspires us to want to make more of our lives.
—Rabbi Daniel Levin, Temple Beth El of Boca Raton

David J. Pollay is my new hero! *The Law of the Garbage Truck* is more than a book; it's a manual for improving the quality of your life.
—Shaun Rawls, New York Tri-State Regional Director and
Operating Partner of The Rawls Group, Keller Williams Realty

David J. Pollay's *The Law of the Garbage Truck* stands out from the hundreds of how-to-live-your-life books: It is backed by the best current research on happiness and well-being . . . readers who seriously commit to these principles will find their lives, their work, and their relationships enriched.
—Raymond D. Fowler, former President of the American Psychological Association

THE
LAW
OF THE
GARBAGE
TRUCK

**How to Respond to People Who Dump on You,
and How to Stop Dumping on Others**

DAVID J. POLLAY

STERLING

New York / London
www.sterlingpublishing.com

STERLING and the distinctive Sterling logo are registered trademarks of
Sterling Publishing Co., Inc.

Library of Congress Cataloging-in-Publication Data Available

2 4 6 8 10 9 7 5 3 1

Published by Sterling Publishing Co., Inc.
387 Park Avenue South, New York, NY 10016
© 2010 by David J. Pollay
Distributed in Canada by Sterling Publishing
c/o Canadian Manda Group, 165 Dufferin Street
Toronto, Ontario, Canada M6K 3H6
Distributed in the United Kingdom by GMC Distribution Services
Castle Place, 166 High Street, Lewes, East Sussex, England BN7 1XU
Distributed in Australia by Capricorn Link (Australia) Pty. Ltd.
P.O. Box 704, Windsor, NSW 2756, Australia

Manufactured in the United States of America
All rights reserved

Sterling ISBN 978-1-4027-7664-9

For information about custom editions, special sales, premium and
corporate purchases, please contact Sterling Special Sales
Department at 800-805-5489 or specialsales@sterlingpublishing.com.

For Dawn, Eliana, and Ariela

For Jerriann and Louis

For Mike

*If there be righteousness in the heart,
there will be beauty in the character.*

*If there be beauty in the character,
there will be harmony in the home.*

*If there be harmony in the home,
there will be order in the nation.*

*If there be order in the nation,
there will be peace in the world.*

—Confucius

Contents

Appendices 205

The Law of the
Garbage Truck

WHAT IF YOU COULD TAKE CONTROL OF YOUR LIFE WITH ONE DECISION?

You can.

I wrote this book to show you how.

My Intention

MY INTENTION WITH THIS BOOK IS BIG.

I want our paths to personal and professional fulfillment to be free of unnecessary distraction. I want us to let the negative things we cannot control in life pass us by. I want us to take the best of what we have and build upon it.

I want us to make the world a better place.

People often ask me, "Who's your audience for *The Law of the Garbage Truck?*"

I answer, "Everyone."

Some smile and say, "Don't you think you should focus on one group?"

"I have," I respond. "The world."

That's my answer.

I WROTE THIS BOOK TO CONNECT WITH EVERYONE. I WANT IT TO REACH people in every country, every city, and every village across our planet. I want *The Law of the Garbage Truck* to help change the way we relate to each other at home and at work. I want us to create and sustain a more productive, compassionate, and peaceful world.

I wrote this book for people who want to take control of their lives. I wrote this book for you and the people you care about.

Our Purpose

IT IS NOT OUR DUTY TO ABSORB THE FRUSTRATIONS, ANXIETIES, AND disappointments of other people. We were not put on earth to carry other people's negative energy, nor were we created to burden others with ours.

We must keep our paths clear of unnecessary limitations and not be discouraged by other people's negative attitudes and actions. And we must not be deterred by our own self-defeating beliefs and behaviors.

We all have a responsibility to discover and live our purpose. We have a right to dream and to pursue what matters most to us.

We can achieve happiness and success by embracing and focusing on what truly matters, personally and professionally. The Law of the Garbage Truck helps pave the way for us to live our best possible lives.

Our Happiness Interrupted

WE ARE MEANT TO DO SOMETHING MEANINGFUL. THE CHALLENGE IS THAT the path forward is not always clear. People and events can get in the way.

Picture your early childhood. For many of us, it was a time of innocence. We had fun. We had friends. We felt loved and happy.

But these joyful times were soon interrupted.

Think about the kids who talked behind your back and who teased or criticized you unfairly. Remember when they told you a friend was mad at you or that someone didn't like you anymore? When you asked why, they didn't give a good answer. It seemed as if you could do nothing to make things better. The power was in their hands. You felt helpless. They were in control.

As we grew older, we hoped that fewer people would have the ability to make us feel vulnerable and angry. But it didn't turn out that way. In fact, a wider circle of people emerged with the capacity to negatively influence our lives.

Everyday encounters with customer service representatives, salesclerks, employees, coworkers, bosses, and customers can derail our days. Their disagreeable behavior can turn a good day into a bad one.

Sure, many of our days are still happy and productive, but it is frustrating when people run across our path and disrupt our well-being. Their negative behavior bothers us and dominates our attention, leaving us with an emotional hangover of bad thoughts and feelings. Why should our happiness and success be susceptible to the unpredictable moods and behaviors of others?

In life we have the opportunity to influence and to be influenced. When someone's example is positive, it's wise to observe, study, and emulate that behavior. However, when someone's behavior is negative, we face a decision. What will we do? Will we accept it, or choose another response? The beauty is that we have a choice. We don't have to be passive receptors of other people's bad attitudes and behaviors. We are here for a greater purpose.

Civility Under Fire

PEOPLE TODAY ARE FRUSTRATED BY THE BEHAVIOR OF OTHERS AND have had enough of insensitive, aggressive, inconsiderate, and sometimes obnoxious behavior. I hear conversations about people's frustration with the incivility of others everywhere—at work, at home, in stores, and in restaurants. Television news programs and talk shows focus on it; radio hosts discuss it with their listeners; writers analyze it in newspapers, magazines, and books; blogs, social networks, and websites are dedicated to it.

It's clear that people are bothered and upset by incivility whenever they experience it—everyday incivility is a burden for everyone. That's why our effort to improve our everyday interactions—public and private—is so important. We can make the world a better place for all of us.

My Mission

MY MISSION IS TO INCREASE HAPPINESS, SUCCESS, AND CIVILITY IN THE world.

My approach starts with each of us. We need to change as individuals before we can prescribe how everyone else should behave. We should not get lost in the debate over who has the right things on their list of dos and don'ts. We can get there later. First, we have to act and make a change that's possible today.

I'm after something fundamental. I want all of us to commit to a profound life philosophy and strategy we can all accept, regardless of our religion, race, nationality, culture, economic status, or educational background.

I want our actions to reflect our commitment. The commitment I'm talking about is following The Law of the Garbage Truck and honoring The Eight No Garbage Trucks! Commitments.

Your Role

THIS BOOK IS BEST READ AND USED AS A PRIVATE JOURNAL, WITH A PEN IN hand. I have written my part. Now, I want you to write yours.

After each chapter, I will ask you a brief question and leave some blank space for your response. As the participants do during the speeches and seminars I present, I want you to write your "top of mind" answers in the spaces provided. Jot down the very first thoughts that pop into your head, without censoring them. All you need are a few minutes to answer each question.

Although I recommend returning to each chapter and reflecting more deeply on your answers, the key to your initial, positive change is the ability to build momentum quickly. So I want you to read a chapter, turn the page, read the question, and write your answer. Then flip the page, and start the next chapter. Get into a rhythm and let your positive energy carry you through the book.

Your Compass

THIS BOOK IS NOT AN ENCYCLOPEDIA. IT IS NOT MY INTENTION TO OFFER tailored responses to every difficult situation you may encounter. Instead, I want to offer a guide that you can use throughout your life. *The Law of the Garbage Truck* is not the only guide you'll ever need, but as a compass it is extremely effective and universally applicable.

Your Questions

YOU WILL HAVE QUESTIONS ALONG THE WAY. YOU WILL WONDER IF THERE are limits to The Law of the Garbage Truck. Write these questions down, but keep going. Keep reading.

You'll find this book is laid out like the building plans of a new home. The early chapters lay a foundation of understanding. Then, with each new chapter, a brick is added to the structure, answering one of your questions, revealing a new insight, and offering another way to apply The Law of the Garbage Truck to your life.

The Eight Commitments of The Law of the Garbage Truck

THIS BOOK WILL TAKE YOU ON A JOURNEY OF DISCOVERY. IN IT YOU WILL learn how to be happier and more successful in your personal and professional life. In fact, your family, colleagues, and society as a whole will benefit from your wholehearted determination to follow The Eight Commitments of The Law of the Garbage Truck:

1. *Do let Garbage Trucks pass you by (Don't let others dump on you):* You do not have to be burdened by the negative things you cannot control. You are free to focus on what matters.

2. *Do let your own Garbage Trucks pass you by (Don't dump on yourself):* Bad memories of your past do not have to weigh you down, and you do not have to be limited by your own negative projections of the future.

3. *Do avoid becoming someone else's Garbage Truck (Don't dump on others):* Your response to people who dump on you does not have to be vengeful and judgmental. Instead, you can give people a chance, stop baiting them, and be more forgiving.

4. *Do help the Garbage Trucks you can (Help others stop dumping):* You acknowledge and celebrate the best in others. You seek opportunities to communicate effectively with everyone.

5. *Do honor your No Garbage Trucks! Pledge:* You do not have to accept garbage and you do not need to spread it. You are not a Garbage Truck.

6. *Do live in The Gratitude Cycle and live free of The Garbage Cycle:* Invest your energy in living a good and meaningful life.

By choosing gratitude, not garbage, you help make the world a better place for everyone.

7. *Do live in a No Garbage Trucks! Zone*: Let everyone know you are committed to living in The Gratitude Cycle and outside the grip of Garbage Trucks. People will know where you stand: You live in a No Garbage Trucks! Zone.

8. *Do work in a No Garbage Trucks! Zone*: By giving your best and expecting the best from others, you contribute to an environment that allows people to enjoy their work, use their strengths, and feel what they do is meaningful.

It's Time

BEFORE WE CONTINUE OUR JOURNEY TOGETHER, I WANT TO THANK YOU FOR being here.

Welcome to *The Law of the Garbage Truck.*

Do Let Garbage Trucks Pass You By

(Don't Let Others Dump on You)

CHAPTER ONE

The Law of the Garbage Truck

He who is slow to anger is better than the mighty,
And he who rules his spirit than he who takes a city.

—Proverbs 16:32

HOW OFTEN DO YOU LET OTHER PEOPLE'S NONSENSE CHANGE YOUR mood? Do you let a bad driver, rude waiter, curt boss, or an insensitive employee ruin your day? Unless you're the Terminator, you're probably set back on your heels. However, the mark of your success is how quickly you can refocus on what's important in your life.

Twenty years ago, I learned this lesson in the back of a New York City taxicab. Here's what happened.

I hopped into a taxi and we took off for Grand Central Station. We were driving in the right-hand lane when, all of a sudden, a black car jumped out of a parking space right in front of us. My taxi driver slammed on his brakes, the car skidded, the tires squealed, and at the very last moment we stopped just one inch from the other car's back end.

I couldn't believe it. But then I couldn't believe what happened next. The driver of the other car—the guy who almost caused a major accident— whipped his head around and started yelling bad words at us. How do I know? Ask any New Yorker. Some words in the City come with a special face. He even threw in a one-finger salute!

But then, here's what really blew me away. My taxi driver just smiled and waved at the guy. And I mean, he was friendly. So I said, "Why did you just do that? That guy could have killed us!" This is when my taxi driver told me what I now call The Law of the Garbage Truck™. He said:

Many people are like garbage trucks. They run around
full of garbage, full of frustration, full of anger, and full of
disappointment. As their garbage piles up, they look for a
place to dump it. And if you let them, they'll dump it on you.
So when someone wants to dump on you, don't take it personally.
Just smile, wave, wish them well, and move on.
Believe me, you'll be happier.

So I started thinking, "How often do I let Garbage Trucks run right over me and dump their garbage? And how often do I take their garbage and spread it to other people at work, at home, or on the street?" It was then that I said, "I don't want their garbage, and I'm not going to spread it anymore."

Taking Control

IN THE MOVIE *THE SIXTH SENSE*, THE LITTLE BOY SAYS, "I SEE DEAD PEOPLE." Well, now *I see Garbage Trucks*. I see the load they're carrying. I see them coming to dump it. And like my taxi driver, I don't take it personally anymore. I just smile, wave, wish them well, and I move on.

When you are able to perceive Garbage Trucks in your life and let them pass by, you immediately increase your happiness, and you keep your path clear for success. The key is to not process Garbage Trucks—don't analyze, contemplate, discuss, or dwell on them—just let them pass by.

One of my favorite football players of all time was Walter Payton. Every day on the football field, after being tackled, he would jump up as quickly as he hit the ground. He never dwelled on a hit. Payton was ready to make the next play his best. The best athletes from around the world in every sport have played this way, and the most inspiring leaders have also lived this way—no matter how many Garbage Trucks they might have faced.

The bottom line is that successful people do not let Garbage Trucks take over their lives.

Florida State University psychologist Roy Baumeister found in his extensive research that you remember bad things more often than good things in your life. You store the bad memories more easily, and you recall them more frequently.

So you must be ready when a Garbage Truck comes your way. You must make room for the good by letting the bad pass you by.

When you commit to The Law of the Garbage Truck, you take control of your life.

Your Action Guide

What about you? What would happen in your life, starting today, if you let more Garbage Trucks pass you by? Write your answer below.

CHAPTER TWO

Let It Pass You By:
Letting Go Is Not Good Enough

That best portion of a good man's life, his little,
nameless, unremembered acts of kindness and of love.

—William Wordsworth

WE ARE OFTEN TOLD THAT WHEN WE'RE FACED WITH ADVERSITY, A CRISIS, OR the inconveniences and frustrations of everyday life, we should learn to "let things go." But that's not the right strategy when we're confronted by Garbage Trucks. Instead, we need to let their negativity "pass us by." There's an important reason to follow this strategy.

To let something go means that you have to take in, absorb, and process the experience first. But, as effective as you may be at eventually letting go, you are still left with the impact and memory of a Garbage Truck.

Over time, the power of that negative memory will diminish if you cease to invest energy in it, but any energy spent processing the original Garbage Truck experience is too much energy diverted from what's important in your life. The more you accumulate these experiences—and then have to let them go later—the more you suffer from the burden of carrying unnecessary anger, frustration, and disappointment.

Daily Frustrations

DAILY CHALLENGES, AND HOW YOU RESPOND TO THEM, MAY BE EVEN more important to your happiness and health than you thought.

Psychologists Susan Folkman and Richard Lazarus found that everyday challenges can have a cumulative negative effect on us greater than some of the worst events of our lives. In their classic book *Stress, Appraisal, and Coping*, Lazarus and Folkman write:

> Our daily lives are filled with far less dramatic stressful experiences that arise from our roles in living. In our research we have referred to these as "daily hassles," the little things that can irritate and distress people.... Although daily hassles are far less dramatic than major changes in life such as divorce or bereavement, they may be even more important in adaptation and health.

How You Pay for It

THINK OF THE ELECTRICITY RUNNING THROUGH YOUR HOME. PLUG IN AN appliance, turn on a light, start a computer: You use energy.

You do the same thing when you plug into other people's negative energy. You absorb it, use it, and then pay for it again and again.

You pay for it by becoming distracted by continual run-ins with Garbage Trucks.

You pay for it with your moods: One moment you feel positive, open-minded, and optimistic, and the next moment you feel frustrated, upset, and defeated.

You pay for it with your health when you suffer the effects of anger, anxiety, and depression.

Whenever you let Garbage Trucks run over you and dump their garbage, you become one of them by absorbing their negative energy.

Garbage Trucks take your intellectual and emotional attention away from what matters most to you. That's why it's so important to let them "pass you by" before you take in their negative attitudes and behaviors, and then later have to "let them go."

In his book *Why Zebras Don't Get Ulcers*, Stanford University biology and neurology researcher Robert Sapolsky writes, "You are penalized if you activate the stress-response too often: You wind up expending so much energy that, as a first consequence, you tire more readily—just plain old everyday fatigue."

Reacting to Garbage Trucks with hostility wears you down and negatively impacts your health. Sapolsky continues, "Hostile people . . . wind up with higher blood pressure and a host of other undesirable features of their cardiovascular systems."

The Key

THINK ABOUT MY TAXI DRIVER IN NEW YORK CITY. WHEN THE CAR PULLED out in front of us, not only did he avoid retaliating, he also didn't get angry. Sure, he didn't approve of the other guy's driving, but he didn't allow himself to descend into a red-faced rage, as many people do. He didn't stop to take on the garbage of the other driver. He just let it pass by. This is the key to happiness and success: Don't take personally what you cannot control. Focus on the good in others and let the bad pass by. I've seen how this has worked in my own family.

Bumpa

FOUR YEARS AFTER MY GRANDMOTHER PASSED AWAY, MY MOTHER'S father—we called him Bumpa—suffered his fourth stroke. With it came the acceleration of dementia.

At times, my grandfather would be completely lucid—his normal, loving, fun self. At other times, my mother saw a side of him that she'd never seen before. In these moments, her father would say things that were insensitive, selfish, and unkind. She knew he was ill, but it still hurt her each time he criticized, yelled, and questioned her love.

On three separate occasions, my parents brought Bumpa from Maine to live in our home in Milwaukee. He had his own bedroom and bathroom. My mom cooked for him, washed his clothes, and cared for him in every way.

But each time, just a few days after his arrival, Bumpa would defiantly say, "Why are you keeping me here? I want to live in my own home!" After the third try, my parents realized that as lonely as my grandfather was in Maine, he would never be happy away from his own home. So they arranged for his return.

The problem was that Bumpa was no longer capable of caring for himself in his home in Maine. My mom and her sister, Marlene, did everything they could to arrange for the extra care my grandfather needed, but it was hard to satisfy him. He just wasn't himself and would often lash out if you didn't do what he wanted. This was hard on everyone.

Mom

ONE WEEKEND, MY PARENTS VISITED ME IN NEW YORK CITY. MY MOTHER WAS particularly distressed about Bumpa and couldn't let go of all the hurt she had been feeling—despite all the books she'd read on spirituality and philosophy, and no matter how often she'd joined me for walks or talked to my father about her experiences. The hurt kept coming from Bumpa— faster than she could let it go.

One night, after dinner, I sat up late talking with Mom. I tried to help her realize how much she had been doing for her father and wrote out a list of everything I could think of that she had done and was doing for him. I wanted her to have a list with her at all times that affirmed the wonderful care she was providing for her father; she needed to know that she was a good daughter. The list was evidence that no matter what my grandfather might say during his dementia-induced episodes, my mother was doing everything she could for him.

It was then that my mother made a change in her life. She knew her father was often not in control of what he thought and said. So, whenever he began one of his uncontrollable rants, she let it "pass by," rather than take it in and later go through the painful process of letting it go. As a result, she did not take her father to task for everything he said. Whenever he acted like a Garbage Truck, she would let him pass by with kindness and love.

In *The How of Happiness*, psychologist Sonja Lyubomirsky writes that while the caregiving role is meaningful, honorable, and important in life, it can also be "detrimental to [the] physical and mental health" of the caregiver. This was certainly true of my mother's experience. But the more she let difficult interactions with her father pass by, the more she could focus on the best of what he still had to give. This allowed Mom the freedom to be the best mother, wife, friend, and daughter she could be: She saw the good in Bumpa and let the rest pass her by.

Your Action Guide

Think about what's going on in your life. Are you taking on the burden of Garbage Trucks now, only to have to let go of the burden later?

Make a commitment this week. Let at least one Garbage Truck pass you by. Then do it again the following week. Write below how good it makes you feel when you do.

CHAPTER THREE

Defensiveness Makes You Vulnerable to Garbage Trucks

A wise man is superior to any insults which can be put upon him,
and the best reply to unseemly behavior is patience and moderation.
—Jean-Baptiste Poquelin Moliere

THE LAW OF THE GARBAGE TRUCK IS ABOUT HUMILITY. NO ONE IS PERFECT. You don't have to defend yourself every time one of your imperfections is pointed out. At the same time there is no need to judge others for their imperfections. Focus on what's good and important in your own relationships and let Garbage Trucks—including those of your own creation—pass you by.

The next time you feel defensive, pause and evaluate where you want to be focused. Are you really being attacked, or is your radar picking up something that will only distract you from what's important?

Remember, you can always return to an issue if you believe it warrants more of your attention. It is easier to revisit an issue in a thoughtful and balanced mood than it is to erase the negative impact of letting a Garbage Truck run over you and unnecessarily provoke your defenses.

Football

DURING A FOOTBALL PRACTICE MY FRESHMAN YEAR IN COLLEGE, I LEARNED what happens when you respond too forcefully to the first thing that triggers your defensiveness. I was a fullback, and my role was to block for the running back.

My coach sent in a play from the sideline. We huddled and the quarterback told us the play. I was supposed to run to my right, pass the line of scrimmage, and block the outside linebacker.

The quarterback called, "Ready!"

We yelled, "Break!" and got in position at the line of scrimmage.

The quarterback barked, "Green 18. Green 18. Set. Hut. Hut. Hut!"

The center snapped the ball to the quarterback. He handed it off to the running back. I started running down the line, looking for the outside linebacker. Then, another defensive player stepped in my path and began to bear down on me. I felt a rush of adrenaline, locked him in my sight, saw the distance between us close, and then I unleashed all my force in a ferocious block, stopping my opponent right where we collided. The running back I was blocking for ran past me and was tackled a few yards away. Just then, I heard the coach yelling from the sideline, "Fullback! Fullback! Where's my fullback?"

I had a delayed reaction. I thought, "Coach can't be yelling for me."

He yelled again, "Pollay, where are you?"

I raised my hand.

"Pollay, what were you doing?" he yelled. He ran up to me, got in my face, and said, "Who were you supposed to hit?"

"The outside linebacker, sir," I said.

"Who did you hit?"

"The defensive end," I said.

"Why did you hit him?" he asked, lowering his voice.

"Because he stepped in front of me," I said.

That's when my coach explained the mistake I had made. He told me I didn't follow the play as planned. My task was to hit the outside linebacker, and another teammate trailing behind me was supposed to pick up the end. I was supposed to run past the end and chase down the linebacker. I didn't, so the linebacker made the tackle.

Too Quick

INITIALLY, I FELT GREAT BECAUSE I MET THE THREAT POSED BY THE DEFENSIVE end. He challenged me and I struck back hard. I had stopped him in his tracks and I felt proud of myself.

But I was wrong. The defense wanted me to hit the end so the linebacker had a free shot at the running back. I fell for their trap.

The coach pointed out that my blocking the wrong guy happens in high school football all the time. In high school, you often block the first person you see. The playbook of your average high school program is not sophisticated.

"Pollay, you're not in high school anymore," Coach said. "Follow the play."

Life

IF YOU LET GARBAGE TRUCKS UNNECESSARILY ACTIVATE YOUR DEFENSES AT every turn, you're not following the play. Instead, you're allowing someone to tease you into a battle that's not yours to fight, thus diverting your energy from the play you're meant to run.

To stay focused on what matters in your life, you must resist the temptation to indulge your ego and strike back at every Garbage Truck that crosses your path. Don't feel good when you hit back at Garbage Trucks. Feel good when you let them pass by.

Your Action Guide

You are vulnerable to the influence of Garbage Trucks when your defenses are always on high alert. When the slightest provocation activates your highest threat levels, you divert energy from the things you really should be focused on.

This week, pay attention to the times you act and feel defensive. Then, assess whether you deployed your defenses appropriately or if you overreacted.

Identify at least one recurring situation in your life where you can reduce your typically defensive reaction. Write this opportunity below.

Then, notice how good it feels to spend less of your life on defensive high alert.

CHAPTER FOUR

Opportunities Arise When We Let Garbage Trucks Pass Us By

Nothing is miserable unless you think it so.
—Anicius Manlius Severinus Boëthius

THE LAST EMPLOYEE ENTERED THE ROOM. THE DOOR CLOSED. PEOPLE WERE seated around the big conference table and against the back and side walls. Everyone looked nervously at the front of the room where I was seated at the head of the table. I checked my watch. It was 9:00 a.m. It was time to start the meeting and tell them what they had dreaded most: They were all losing their jobs.

Two months earlier my boss had warned me about this day and about taking this job.

The Backstory

I WAS WORKING FOR GLOBAL PAYMENT SYSTEMS, A JOINT VENTURE formed the year before by MasterCard and National Data Corporation. The new company had two customer service centers: MasterCard's high-performing center in St. Louis and National Data Corporation's center in Atlanta, which was struggling. At the time Global Payment Systems was formed, I was a director of planning and administration for MasterCard in New York. Shortly after the new company was launched, I accepted an offer to join Global Payment Systems. I began commuting from New York to Atlanta to help the leadership team turn the operations around. Six months later I moved to Atlanta.

I was the second in command of the Atlanta center when my boss told me that corporate was going to consolidate the St. Louis and Atlanta centers in order to cut costs. All customer service would then be provided out of St. Louis. She said the current director—who had only recently taken over the center—had left the company for another opportunity. My boss said I could take over the Atlanta center, but recommended against it. She suggested I could take a transfer instead because running the center would be a thankless job, and the employees would direct their anger at me when they learned that the center was closing. Morale would sink and service levels would plummet. In short, nothing good would happen.

Making matters worse, it would take four months to build the capacity in the St. Louis center to handle the additional call volume and learn how to service the products we supported in Atlanta. So, while I was charged with telling employees that soon they would be without a job, I would also have to ask them to stay long enough to train the St. Louis representatives. This would not be easy.

I took the job anyway, knowing it would be hard, but I believed we could do something special as a team. My boss backed my decision, gave me the resources I needed, and enlisted the talent of the top leaders in St. Louis. Meanwhile, the employees' concerns were real and had to be addressed. For one, they needed compensation plans and career counseling to help manage the change and find meaningful work before their time at the center came to an end. And I knew they needed one more thing. As a team and as individuals, we had to focus on what we could control—putting ourselves in the best position to do what was right for both the business and our careers.

The Challenge

WE HAD FOUR MONTHS TO KEEP OUR SERVICE LEVELS UP IN ATLANTA WHILE simultaneously finding places for nearly one hundred people inside and outside the company. If we worked together, we could surpass all our service level goals—and even achieve record performance levels—in the midst of a corporate shutdown. Employers would not only see outstanding performance, they would see outstanding character.

I knew our employees could find their way to happiness if they believed our mission was important; their role was valuable; and their work was enjoyable, especially in the midst of uncertainty in their professional lives—they would be better positioned to get a new job quickly.

Research in psychology confirms that happier people enjoy more successful career transitions. In their paper "Does Happiness Promote Career Success," psychologists Julia Boehm and Sonja Lyubomirsky write, "Happy people are less likely to lose their jobs and to be unemployed than less happy people. . . . Furthermore, if a happy person does happen to be unemployed, he or she is likely to find a new job more quickly than an unhappy unemployed person." The researchers also note, "Even before a happy person obtains a job, he or she is more likely to receive a second interview than a less happy peer."

The Meeting

I LOOKED AROUND THE ROOM ONE MORE TIME, GLANCED AT MY NOTES, looked up, and started talking. I told the employees about the cost cutting measures the company was taking, and that corporate had chosen our center to close. I told them I had been given a chance to leave, but I decided to stay because I believed in our team.

I was honest. I told them that corporate believed that after the meeting ended, we would go back to our desks and answer less than half of the calls that came into the center for the rest of the day. It would be a mess, and it would stay that way until we closed the center four months later.

I told them we were better than that. I said I believed we could achieve our goals and find new jobs. It would be a big task, but we could do it. The key was for us to focus on what was important and to let the negative things we could not control pass us by.

People would spread rumors. We would let them pass by. People would complain. We would let them pass by. People would advise us to quit, but we would let them pass by. People would say that we should spite the company and work slowly, and we'd let them pass by, too. When people would try to dump their garbage on us, we would let it pass by.

We were on a mission.

What Happened?

PEOPLE CRIED, GOT UPSET, AND ASKED LOTS OF QUESTIONS AT THE meeting. After all the questions had been asked and answered, we left the conference room and went back to the phones.

I watched people settle back into their cubicles and put on their headsets. I looked at the calls in the customer queue monitor. During the time we had been off the floor, the calls had piled up. Twenty-five calls were in queue. I knew that was a lot to overcome and looked away.

One of my supervisors tapped me on the shoulder.

"David, take a look at the monitor," he said.

I turned back and saw that there were only sixteen calls in queue. I stared at the monitor. Like a New Year's Eve countdown, the calls in waiting were steadily dropping. Our employees were serving our customers.

Throughout the day, call after call was answered. People delayed their breaks to stay on the phones. They reached out to help each other resolve difficult customer issues and worked quickly after each call to update our customer records in the database so that they could answer the next call in line. It was like that all day.

Before I left that evening, I looked at our statistics. Corporate said we would answer only half our calls, but we did better than that. In fact, we answered 96 percent of them—that was 1 percent better than the industry standard for service excellence.

The next four months continued this way. We set service level records in the center and helped almost all of our employees find jobs inside and outside of the company. But it was not easy.

We were not the only ones under stress. Our sales team worried about their customers getting service. Our marketing team was anxious about the support of their products. Good people under stress can easily become Garbage Trucks.

We did our best to listen to complaints without taking them personally if they were delivered in a negative manner. We didn't always succeed. Sometimes we didn't hear the most important information because we let ourselves be triggered by someone's negative attitude. The process of downsizing a company often draws employees into a downward spiral, where their attitudes, behavior, and performance suffer. In our case, people rallied: More often than not we made the most of a difficult situation by listening for what we could control, acting on it, and letting what we could not influence pass us by.

The Rest of the Story

PEOPLE OFTEN ASK ME HOW I BECAME YAHOO!'S FIRST DIRECTOR OF Customer Care. The answer is that my journey to Yahoo! began when I decided to stay with the Atlanta customer service center and lead it during a difficult time. It was a decision I never anticipated having to make when I moved from New York to Atlanta earlier that year. I had relocated to help improve a center, not to close it. But I saw the consolidation as an opportunity to help people achieve something important when the odds were against them. Things weren't perfect, but the results were enough for Global Payment Systems to celebrate our achievement, and for Yahoo! to take notice of my work.

Yahoo! felt that if I could run a customer care center successfully during a consolidation, I could build a customer care organization in a company on the rise.

Your Action Guide

Some of our best opportunities appear when we let Garbage Trucks pass us by.

Think about what's happening in your life now.

In what areas of your life are you allowing Garbage Trucks to get in the way of pursuing opportunities? Choose one, and write below how you will free yourself of the influence of the Garbage Trucks who are holding you back.

Feel the energy you get when you make room for an opportunity in your life.

CHAPTER FIVE

Do You Have the Guts?

*You gain strength, courage, and confidence by every experience
in which you really stop to look fear in the face. You are able to say
to yourself, "I have lived through this horror. I can take the next thing
that comes along." You must do the thing you think you cannot do.*

—Eleanor Roosevelt

BRANCH RICKEY WAS LOOKING FOR THE RIGHT PERSON—SOMEONE WHO had extraordinary character with "guts enough not to fight back"; who could stay focused on the goal, not retaliation; and who would fight for advancement, not payback.

Rickey's search was conducted across the United States, Cuba, Mexico, Puerto Rico, and Venezuela. He took his time—as long as needed—to conduct the search. The right person had to be found.

And then one day it happened. Rickey found the man he had been looking for and invited him to Brooklyn for a meeting.

"They'll taunt and goad you," Rickey told the man. "They'll do anything to make you react." He wanted to be sure the man was strong enough to carry out the mission, which required that "he had to be able to stand up in the face of merciless persecution and not retaliate. On the other hand, he had to be a contradiction in human terms: He still had to have spirit . . . once having proved his ability . . . he had to be able to cast off humility and stand up as a full-fledged participant whose triumph did not carry the poison of bitterness."

The Man

JACKIE ROBINSON WAS THE MAN BRANCH RICKEY HAD BEEN SEARCHING FOR.
Rickey was the president of the Brooklyn Dodgers professional baseball
team. Robinson was a player for the Kansas City Monarchs, a professional
baseball team in the Negro League.

Branch Rickey's plan to break the color barrier in professional baseball
was later called "The Noble Experiment," and Jackie Robinson was the
player chosen to make it happen.

Robinson's first year in the league exposed him to a torrent of cruelty,
hatred, and mistreatment, just as Rickey had predicted. Millions were allied
against him: Fans taunted and booed him in the stadiums, players ignored
and isolated him in the locker room, and hotels refused to accommodate
him on road trips. Hate mail was sent. Threat mail arrived. And all the while
Jackie Robinson played baseball.

Robinson had made a pledge and he honored it. It kept him centered
and gave him strength, as Robinson recalled in his autobiography, *I Never
Had It Made*: "Could I turn the other cheek? I didn't know how I would do
it. Yet I knew that I must. I had to do it for so many reasons. For black youth,
for my mother, for Rae, for myself. I had already begun to feel I had to do it
for Branch Rickey."

Bearing Witness

THE ROAD WAS LONELY, BUT ROBINSON WAS NOT ALONE. HIS WIFE,
Rachel, supported him, Branch Rickey stood by him—and there were
others, too, who had the courage and moral strength to stand up for
Robinson.

No matter how strong you are, there are times when you need
someone else to stand up for you. When Garbage Trucks number in the
thousands or more, you can't win alone. Someone has to be your witness
and help you on your journey.

Pee Wee Reese was such a witness for Jackie Robinson. Reese, a future
Hall of Fame shortstop, was being heckled in a game in Boston. Robinson
was playing second base. Here's how Robinson describes the moment in
his autobiography:

They were riding him about being a Southerner and playing ball with a black man. Pee Wee didn't answer them. Without a glance in their direction, he left his position and walked over to me. He put his hand on my shoulder and began talking to me. His words weren't important. I don't even remember what he said. It was the gesture of comradeship and support that counted. As he stood talking with me with a friendly arm around my shoulder, he was saying loud and clear, "Yell. Heckle. Do anything you want. We came here to play baseball."

Reese answered the Garbage Trucks that day by smiling, waving, and wishing them well. And Jackie Robinson had a witness. He was not alone.

Reese knew what Robinson and Rickey knew. The Dodgers would win if they let the Garbage Trucks pass them by, and if they kept their attention, energy, and spirit focused on their mission.

Stanley Woodward, the sports editor for the *New York Herald Tribune*, was another witness. Woodward had learned of a plot by the St. Louis Cardinals to stage a last-minute protest strike against a game in which Robinson was scheduled to play. If he played, the Cardinals would refuse to take the field and their action could set a series of strikes in motion that would embolden the enemies of integrated baseball.

Woodward wouldn't have it. The story he printed in the *Tribune* about the plot took the power of secrecy and surprise away from the Cardinals and exposed their plan before they could enact it.

Woodward could have sat by silently. Instead, he chose to speak up. So did Ford Frick, commissioner of the National League, who acted forcefully when he learned of the St. Louis plot against Robinson and the Dodgers. He warned the Cardinals in no uncertain terms that if they acted on their plan they would pay dearly:

I do not care if half the league strikes. Those who do it will encounter quick retribution. They will be suspended and I don't care if it wrecks the National League for five years. This is the United States of America, and one citizen has as much right to play as another. The National League will go down the line with Robinson whatever the consequence.

The strike never happened. Frick's forceful stance helped avert a devastating strike. Jackie Robinson had another witness. He was not alone.

Jackie Robinson succeeded because he had "guts enough not to fight back," yet he was not to be denied. He let Garbage Trucks pass by. He also succeeded because he had the support of Branch Rickey, Pee Wee Reese, Stanley Woodward, Ford Frick, and other courageous men and women who were not deterred or intimidated by Garbage Trucks. They did what they believed was right.

Courage

WHAT ABOUT YOUR LIFE? WILL YOU PERSEVERE WHEN GARBAGE TRUCKS rally against you? Will you keep your attention focused on what you can control—and let Garbage Trucks pass by so you can accomplish your mission?

And what about the lives of others? Will you have the courage to be a Branch Rickey, Pee Wee Reese, Stanley Woodward, or Ford Frick in someone else's life? Will you be a witness and stand up for what is right?

Your Action Guide

Jackie Robinson faced a challenge greater than most of us could imagine. Millions of people he didn't know tried to derail his dream and the dreams of millions of others. He did not respond to every Garbage Truck; he let them pass by, and he accomplished his mission. He made history.

What about you?

What do you value enough that you won't let Garbage Trucks get in the way of achieving your dreams?

Write your answer below in three to four sentences.

Do Let Your Own Garbage Trucks Pass You By

(Don't Dump on Yourself)

THE SECOND LESSON TO LEARN ABOUT THE LAW OF THE GARBAGE
Truck is that other people are not the only ones who bring garbage into
our lives—we create plenty of our own negativity that stirs memories of
our past and makes us fearful of what we imagine awaits us in the
future. Garbage Trucks have the power to lock us into self-defeating
habits and thought patterns that keep us from living our best possible
lives. Now it's time to take that power away from them.

CHAPTER SIX

How to Let Garbage Trucks in Your Memory Pass By

The sun is new every day.

—Heraclitus

EVENTS IN OUR LIVES, AND OUR INTERPRETATIONS OF THEM, PLAY LIKE a continuous stream of short videos in our minds. The video projector is always running, and many of the videos we view on the screen feature Garbage Trucks. We've stored a video in our memory of almost everyone who has ever hurt, embarrassed, worried, insulted, frustrated, angered, or disappointed us.

Psychologist Roy Baumeister and his colleagues at Florida State University write in their paper "Bad is Stronger than Good":

> The greater power of bad events over good ones is found in everyday events. . . . Bad emotions . . . and bad feedback have more impact than good ones, and bad information is processed more thoroughly than good. . . . Bad impressions and bad stereotypes are quicker to form' and more resistant to change than good ones.

Reliving the Past

HERE'S THE CHALLENGE: THE BAD VIDEOS OF YOUR LIFE CAN START PLAYING at the slightest suggestion or provocation. One moment you're fine, and the next you're thinking about something bad that happened a long time ago.

When negative memories are invoked, we often indulge in looking for new meanings in them. But as we contemplate and re-analyze these memories, our bodies respond and we often feel the experience as if it were happening right now. Our gut tightens, our breathing becomes shallow, our body tenses, and we take on the mood of the original event.

Let me give you an example of this phenomenon, a positive one. Consider for a moment a wonderful event in your life, such as the day you graduated from college, got your first job, or met your first love. Now, pause, close your eyes, and remember this moment in as much detail as possible. Take a minute to enjoy that memory.

How did that memory make you feel? Did you smile, laugh, or just feel good in some way? What was it like to reconnect with that wonderful event? What did you see? What did you smell? What did you taste?

Suffering the Past

NOW, IF WE WERE ABLE TO SAVOR THE GOOD MEMORIES MORE REGULARLY, we would be happier. The challenge is that our minds tend to search for and focus on reruns of the bad things in our past, rather than the good things. As a consequence, we suffer run-ins with Garbage Trucks over and over again.

As we engage these bad memories, and as they pass through our consciousness—when we wake up, go to bed, experience stress, or even when we're in the middle of a happy time—we strengthen them. We feel the initial mood of disappointment, anxiety, and doubt all over again. By energizing these old memories with new thinking, we give them additional importance in our lives.

Scientists have reported that our memories are really just memories of the last memory of an experience. So every time you recall an event in your life, you are not going back to review the original footage, but instead you are referencing your last recollection of the event. In his book *Stumbling on Happiness*, the Harvard psychology researcher Daniel Gilbert writes how memory is not the objective reporter and historian we think it is.

Remembering an experience feels a lot like opening a drawer and retrieving a story that was filed away on the day it was written, but . . . that feeling is one of our brain's most sophisticated illusions. Memory is not a dutiful scribe that keeps a complete transcript of our experiences, but a sophisticated editor that clips and saves key elements of an experience and then uses these elements to rewrite the story each time we ask to reread it.

Basically, we remember events selectively and not very accurately. We rewrite our memories both good and bad.

Just a False Alarm

THINGS GET EVEN MORE COMPLEX WHEN WE EXAMINE THE BASIC NATURE OF the brain.

Our brain automatically tries to keep us safe. We are wired not to hurt or kill ourselves. The challenge is that our brain has an alarm system that can be hypersensitive. It often sends us physical and emotional alerts to warn us of problems that pose no real threat. As a result, we are left to respond to psychological and physical false alarms.

The Fear Trigger

BRUCE PERRY, THE FORMER CHIEF OF PSYCHIATRY AT TEXAS CHILDREN'S Hospital, writes in the book *Splintered Reflections*:

The remarkable capacity of the brain to take a specific event and generalize, particularly with regard to threatening stimuli, makes humans vulnerable to the development of "false" associations and false generalizations from a specific traumatic event to other non-threatening situations.

Essentially, traumatic events in our lives that have long since passed can continue to exact their toll by triggering fear in us—even when there is no longer anything to fear.

Waking Up Happy

MOST DAYS I WAKE UP FEELING HAPPY. WHY? THE ANSWER IS SIMPLE: I GET to wake up each morning to the warm embrace of my wife, Dawn, and I cherish the morning routine of getting our little girls ready for school. Even on days when I get up a little tired, I still feel happy because I am focused on what I care about.

Waking Up Unhappy

CONTRAST THE TYPICAL HAPPY MORNINGS AT HOME WITH THE DAYS I'M traveling on business: It is not uncommon for me to wake up with old memories, a thought, or a feeling I cannot explain. Some of these thoughts are negative—Garbage Trucks from my past. Then my groggy morning brain automatically starts searching for evidence of whether I'm still under the influence of those negative memories and thoughts. And, if I'm not mindful, I will find some shred of evidence to prove that they are somehow still important and playing a role in my life. The result is that the initial bad memory or thought captures my attention and then sets the tone for the start of my day.

What Can You Do?

THE FIRST KEY IS TO RECOGNIZE THAT YOUR BRAIN WILL CONTINUE TO SEND subconscious warning signals every day of your life. The second key is to understand that your initial emotional reaction to these warnings may also be subconsciously activated by the memories your brain associates with the alarm. In his book *The Happiness Hypothesis*, the University of Virginia psychology researcher Jonathan Haidt writes about the subconscious processes of the brain: "Automatic processes generate thousands of thoughts and images every day, often through random association. The ones that get stuck are the ones that particularly shock us, the ones we try to suppress or deny."

The third and final key is to realize that there is no need to engage all these negative memories. We do not have to reflect on and analyze them each time they surface. These three keys unlock the door to our happiness, freeing us from the Garbage Trucks of our past.

A Time to "Smile, Wave, Wish Them Well, and Move On"

THANKFULLY, WE NOW KNOW THE POWER OF APPLYING THE LAW OF THE Garbage Truck to bad memories. You do not need to suppress or deny your bad memories and negative thoughts when they appear, "just smile, wave, wish them well, and move on."

There comes a time when you must acknowledge certain memories as Garbage Trucks, and it's up to you to let those bad memories pass you by. Don't let them diminish your joy, your confidence, or your belief in what is good and possible in your life.

Your Action Guide

Most of us have at least one Garbage Truck memory that periodically surfaces and changes our mood negatively. Do you have one? How does this memory continue to bother you? Write your answer below.

Make a promise to yourself. The next time this Garbage Truck memory appears, just smile, wave, wish it well, and let it pass by. When you do this, concentrate on how good it makes you feel to let the memory pass you by. Hold on to that feeling.

CHAPTER SEVEN

How to Let Garbage Trucks in Your Future Pass By

There is only one way to happiness, and that is to cease
worrying about things which are beyond the power of our will.
—Epictetus

INEVITABLY, WE ALL SPEND TIME THINKING ABOUT THE FUTURE—TO COMMIT to the success we seek and to prepare for the obstacles we may encounter. Even considering the worst possible consequences of our actions can be a thoughtful strategy in life and business. It is important to be prepared for what could happen. But ruminating about the possible arrival of a Garbage Truck never helps us accomplish anything. It takes our attention away from enjoying what we have today, addressing the problems we face, and planning for what we want tomorrow.

A Very Bad Week

I LEARNED NOT TO OBSESS OVER THE POTENTIAL APPEARANCE OF GARBAGE Trucks in my future after one of the most disappointing weeks of my life. It happened at a time and place where so many of us are vulnerable to a sea of setbacks and disappointments: college.

I was a young kid from Wisconsin—away from home for the first time— and I was trying to make it through my first semester at Yale. Things got off to a bumpy start in the large auditorium in Harkness Hall where I was taking my economics midterm exam with about four hundred other students. As I got up to hand in my exam, I heard a "Whoaaaaa" from hundreds of students who were looking at me in awe. I left a three-hour exam in less than forty minutes, and it was clear that my peers were blown away by how smart I must be to have finished so quickly. Little did they know that two days later my economics professor would return my exam with a score of 6 out of 100. I had left my exam early because I didn't know what I was doing! And that was just the beginning of my week.

The next day I had better news: I'd upped my performance from an F in economics to a D+ in astronomy. The week continued its downward slide on the football field.

My parents and younger brother were making the trip from Milwaukee to New Haven to watch me play football in our second game of the season, but during practice the day before they arrived, I made a wrong turn and tore my hamstring. My family made it to the game, only to see me standing on the sidelines leaning on crutches, instead of running with a football.

Finally, the week came to an end with my new girlfriend telling me, "David, I'm 'pre-engaged' to be married." I had no idea what "pre-engaged" meant, but I knew it couldn't be good . . . for me, anyway.

Failure

UP TO THAT POINT IN MY LIFE, I CONSIDERED MYSELF OPTIMISTIC. SURE, I HAD doubts, but mostly I worked through them. Now, things seemed different. Academically, I was in trouble. My dream of playing college football might be over, and my new girlfriend was really not my girlfriend.

I imagined going back to Milwaukee as a failure. I pictured people telling me that I wasn't good enough to play college football and that I wasn't cut out for an Ivy League education. I was afraid that my classmates and teammates would avoid me, and I was worried that my professors wouldn't make time to help me.

In short, I was imagining a whole convoy of Garbage Trucks in my future. The more I focused on the negative things that people might say and do, the more distorted my vision became of what was positive and possible.

The "Jack Story"

THAT'S WHEN MY DAD HELPED ME SEE THE GARBAGE TRUCKS I WAS imagining in my future. He told me an old story to make the point. It's a version of the classic comedy routine by Danny Thomas.

A guy is driving through the desert when one of his tires blows out. He gets out of his car and pops open the trunk to look for a spare tire and a jack. He sees the spare, but there's no jack. "Oh no!" he yells. "I've got to walk back to the gas station I passed five miles ago!"

So he starts walking. "I hope he has a jack," he says to himself. Half way there he mumbles anxiously, "He better have a jack." When he's almost there he growls, "That guy better let me use his jack!"

Minutes later he finally arrives at the gas station. He's hot. He's frustrated. He's fuming. He sees the station owner in the garage and he walks up to him and says, "Hey buddy, you can forget it! You can keep your stinkin' jack!"

He turns around and marches five miles back to his car . . . with no jack.

My dad then looked at me, smiled, and said, "Don't build a 'Jack Story.'"

He believed you gain nothing by obsessing over the worst things that could happen in a situation. Why invest all your energy in imagining only scenarios that end poorly? Not only do you make yourself feel terrible, you still have to deal with the problem at hand.

Psychologists Karen Reivich and Andrew Shatte write about the perils of catastrophic thinking in their book *The Resilience Factor*. "For many people," they write, "their anxiety takes over and they catastrophize—they dwell on a current adversity and within a few minutes have imagined a chain of disastrous events stretching into the future."

Reivich and Shatte outline an effective five-step method for countering catastrophic thinking. Here's what they suggest:

1. Name your adversity and the worst-case things you believe could happen as a result.

2. Evaluate the probability that each of these events will happen. You'll see the odds are long against any of them coming to pass.

3. Next, think of the best-case scenarios possible. They should be so unrealistic that they make you smile or even laugh. You want to break your "doom and gloom" thinking.

4. Now that you've plotted the extreme cases—you've identified the worst and the best results possible—focus on the most likely outcomes of the adversity.

5. Then, with your newfound perspective, come up with a solution to remedy the problem.

The bottom line is that we all experience setbacks. Unfortunately, we often forget to look at these situations like the even-tempered Sergeant Joe "Just the Facts" Friday on the classic 1950s television show *Dragnet*. Instead, we turn into Chicken Little and say, "The sky is falling!"

Martin Seligman, the psychologist best known for his research on learned helplessness and learned optimism and for his role in founding the science of positive psychology, believes that pessimism rarely serves us well. Seligman summarizes the results of more than twenty years of research on pessimism in his book *Authentic Happiness*: "Pessimists . . . are up to eight times more likely to become depressed when bad events happen," he writes. "They do worse at school, sports and most jobs than their talents augur. They have worse physical health and shorter lives. They have rockier interpersonal relations, and they lose American presidential elections to their more optimistic opponents."

It's Natural . . . Just Let Them Pass By

WE KNOW EVENTS IN OUR LIVES TRIGGER NEGATIVE, UNHELPFUL THOUGHTS. This happens to all of us—it's natural, and it's part of the human condition. The key is to not fixate on these thoughts when they appear, quite simply because it is a waste of energy to invest in fighting or blocking these unwanted thoughts.

It is better to turn your attention to the future you want and to a list of more likely positive scenarios. You can focus your energy on a plan to achieve the results you desire. Then, if you are triggered to think negatively about your future, you can redirect your focus to the well-grounded, optimistic, and realistic expectations of what you intend to achieve.

Yale Part II

DURING THE DIFFICULT, EARLY DAYS FOR ME AT YALE, MY FATHER HELPED me break out of a whirlwind of imagining Garbage Trucks in my future, and I started to focus on what I could control. I started by asking for advice from my professors, and they gave it to me: I moved up a few rows in class and I did my homework. And while it didn't work out with my girlfriend and I never became a football star in college, I did turn my grades around. Eventually I majored in economics, and I was honored to carry our college banner at graduation.

You gain nothing by continually replaying your worst visions of how people might be unkind, unhelpful, and unfriendly to you; this only creates Garbage Trucks where they don't exist. By smiling, waving, wishing them well, and moving on, you are free to focus on what really matters.

Your Action Guide

Think about your personal and professional future. What Garbage Trucks have you been inventing? Write your answer below.

The next time you find yourself obsessing over the worst possible scenarios, follow The Law and just smile, wave, and let those scenarios pass by in your mind. Then, take immediate action—implement a part of your plan—to create the future you want.

CHAPTER EIGHT

Living the Words

The only unavoidable choice was whether or not
to have Parkinson's. Everything else was up to me.

—Michael J. Fox

ATHAN RAY, A VETERAN POLICE OFFICER OF NINETEEN YEARS, LIVES IN Brisbane, Australia. He is happily married, loves his wife and two kids, and enjoys his job.

Athan recently wrote a letter to his children, Lauren and Andrew. He wanted to tell them how much he loves them; the hopes he has for them; what he admires in them; and how he will always—in some way—support them. It's a beautiful letter. I know because Athan asked me to read it. However, his wife, Lisa, has not read the letter because it's too hard for her to think about the reasons Athan wrote it.

Athan has a disease so rare that his doctors aren't certain what it is, although they think it may be cerebral lymphomatoid granulomatosis. When lymphomatoid granulomatosis (LYG) remains localized in the brain, preliminary research suggests it's treatable, but the long-term prognosis is unknown. However, if LYG spreads to other organs, the mortality rate is ominously high.

The Journey

IT ALL BEGAN WHEN ATHAN SUFFERED A SEIZURE IN 2007. HIS DOCTORS thought he had a brain tumor and scheduled him for brain surgery. What they found appeared to be meningoencephalitis, an infection or inflammation of the brain. Doctors removed the infected area, and after a long recovery, Athan returned to work where he collapsed three months later. Brain scans revealed three new lesions in his brain.

After a second surgery and a biopsy, the doctors came up with an unconfirmed diagnosis of cerebral lymphomatoid granulomatosis.

Athan returned to work once again, battle-worn, but hopeful. The lesions disappeared.

Two years later, however, in November 2009, during one of Athan's periodic brain scans, doctors found three new lesions. Because he wasn't experiencing any symptoms, the doctors decided to monitor his condition before determining what to do next. They didn't have to wait long.

On January 27, 2010, Athan suffered another seizure. This time he fell into a coma. Eight hours later Athan returned to consciousness.

There was good news. Athan suffered no brain damage during the seizure and coma. More good news: The three lesions on Athan's brain had resolved and no longer appeared on the brain scan. However, to protect against future seizures, Athan was put on another antiseizure drug.

Athan is tired, but he's doing better. "Do the doctors ever talk about a prognosis?" I asked him.

"They have just as many questions as I have," he said. "They have no real idea how this is going to pan out. It could develop and spread to other parts of my body and become more destructive. So, as you can imagine, each scan can lead us in a new direction. It is certainly a nerve-racking time. The doctors worry that if they pursue the wrong treatment, the effects could be far worse."

Worry

"WHAT DO YOU DO WHEN YOU BEGIN TO WORRY?" I ASKED ATHAN.

"One thing I have learned to expect is that worry is a completely normal and expected response," Athan said. "Being able to identify when it becomes excessive and detrimental is the key."

Athan's pragmatic outlook is supported by the work of Edward Hallowell, a psychiatrist and former instructor at Harvard Medical School. In his book *Worry*, Hallowell distinguishes between what he calls "'good worry' (The plane might be late. I'd better call the airport.) and 'toxic worry' (The plane may have crashed. I'd better sit here and be miserable until I meet the plane.)." Hallowell emphasizes how important it is to act quickly to ensure that good worry does not turn to toxic worry. "There is a window of opportunity—it lasts perhaps as long as a minute—during which you can sever the tentacle of a toxic worry before it grips you totally. For most people, once it gets a tight grip, it lasts for hours, even days or weeks. To cut it off immediately, you must take decisive action."

Athan told me that after reading "The Law of the Garbage Truck," he realized he was generating a lot of his own toxic worry:

My garbage wasn't coming from other people as much as I was creating it myself because of my disease. As you can imagine you have a range of emotions: anger, self-pity, sadness, and a sense of loss. But I realized for my body to get better, I needed to redirect my attention from negative ideas and thoughts to the positive and what I could do. I could not afford to take on more garbage.

What you have to focus on when you're in my circumstance is how to handle the moments when you start to dump on yourself. How do you smile, wave, and let your unhelpful thoughts pass by? First, you must realize you're being a Garbage Truck. Second, you have to look in the mirror and tell yourself that you are not going to be your own Garbage Truck.

Centering

ATHAN IS RARELY FREE FROM THE REALITY OF HIS CONDITION. HE ADHERES to a regular medication regimen, exercises to keep up his strength, chooses foods wisely, and makes frequent visits to his doctors. With so many constant concerns about his health, it would be easy for Athan to be distracted from all the other responsibilities in his life.

"What do you do to stay centered and positive?" I asked Athan.

"I play trains and cars with the kids. I get down on the ground and play," he said. "I remind myself that I still have so much to be thankful for. I laugh with my friends and I think about how much stronger I will be once I come out on the other side of this. I keep telling myself that some questions like 'why me?' have no answer, and I have to accept that. I know that it is just as easy to create your own garbage as it is for someone to dump it on you. So, I like to visualize myself getting better."

Athan continued, "The Law helps me cope when I'm angry, fearful, anxious, sad, and depressed, to name some of the emotions I feel at times. I remind myself that I am not a Garbage Truck. I don't need all those negative emotions piling up inside of me. They don't serve any purpose. When I let the garbage pass by, I'm not weighed down by the things that don't help me."

If anyone could be justified in being worried and depressed, it's Athan. Instead, he appreciates his life as never before. He knows something we'll all find out one day: A long life is not guaranteed. Our time is uncertain. With that knowledge, Athan chooses to neither accept nor dump garbage. It's one of the important things he can control.

Athan wrote a letter to his children. Now, he's living the words.

Your Action Guide

Athan understands the reality of what we all face: It's impossible for us to foresee everything that is to come. So Athan is mindful to focus on his blessings and on what he can control, not the worst-case scenarios of an uncertain future.

What are you worrying about in your future that is taking away from your life now? Write your answer below in a few sentences.

What action can you take to prepare for the future so that you can stay centered on the present? List below the practical things that you can do to ensure a better future than the one you're worried about. Follow up by implementing one of the things on your list this week.

Then, when disturbing thoughts still come—and they will—know that you are preparing for the best future possible, and then smile, wave, and let those thoughts of Garbage Trucks in your future pass by. Notice how much better you feel when you do.

Do Avoid Becoming Someone Else's Garbage Truck

(Don't Dump on Others)

HERE'S THE BIG WAKE-UP CALL. WE ALL ARE GARBAGE TRUCKS AT ONE time or another—some of us more often than others. It happens when we carry frustration, anger, disappointment, anxiety, and bitterness in our lives. When our burden becomes too heavy, we do what Garbage Trucks do: We dump and spread it around to others. But we can stop doing this. We do not have to become Garbage Trucks.

CHAPTER NINE

Revenge Does Not Pay

Nothing on earth consumes a man more
quickly than the passion of resentment.

—Friedrich Nietzsche

MANY PEOPLE SPEND THEIR LIVES TRYING TO GET BACK AT GARBAGE TRUCKS. They feel abused, challenged, or violated after being run over by one, so their mission is to hit back as soon as they can. They often think about what they *could have said* or *should have done* and fantasize about revenge.

They become movie directors. They imagine a scene where they get to talk like the hero of a big-budget action movie: "You just dumped garbage on the wrong guy." Then, in their dream scene, they stick it to the person who hurt them. And, even better, they watch it all in slow motion to extend the joy of getting even. The scene ends with them walking triumphantly into the distance with victory music playing in the background. Why? They just carried out "justice."

Bad for Your Health

REALITY PLAYS OUT DIFFERENTLY THAN IN THE MOVIES, HOWEVER. IN HIS book *Authentic Happiness*, positive psychology cofounder Martin Seligman speaks directly to the pitfalls of lashing back—or even ruminating about lashing back—at people who have crossed us:

> *Dwelling on trespass and the expression of anger produces more*
> *cardiac disease and more anger . . . The overt expression of*

hostility turns out to be the real culprit in the Type-A-heart attack link . . . In one study, 255 medical students took a personality test that measured overt hostility. As physicians twenty-five years later, the angriest had roughly five times as much heart disease as the least angry ones. In another study, men who had the highest risk of later heart attacks were just the ones with more explosive voices, more irritation when forced to wait, and more outwardly directed anger.

Incivility on the Road

IN A PAPER PUBLISHED IN THE *JOURNAL OF AGGRESSION AND VIOLENT Behavior*, two psychologists from The State University of New York at Albany, Tara Galovski and Edward Blanchard, consider a particularly perilous and common form of revenge: road rage. The researchers note how elevated stress leads to increased fatalities on the roadways: "Research has shown that drivers who are currently experiencing major life stressors are five times more likely to cause fatal accidents than drivers who were relatively free from serious life stressors."

All you have to do is drive on the highway for a week to see how people try to teach each other a lesson. Some people won't let driving transgressions pass them by and seem to obsess over them. They feel they have to hold *all* guilty drivers accountable for each new infraction, no matter how minor. When someone makes a bad move driving, they lay on the horn, tailgate, yell, wave wildly, or cut the person off in return. This type of behavior is not only bad for their health, as the research confirms, it also puts other people at risk. And their focus on revenge ratchets up the potential harm to everyone around them.

The psychology researchers Brad Bushman, William Pedersen, Eduardo Vasquez, Norman Miller, and Angela Bonacci conducted three studies on the effects of ruminating about a provocation in our lives. Bushman and his colleagues were particularly interested in a psychological phenomenon called "displaced aggression."

In simple terms, displaced aggression boils down to taking out your frustration on someone else; you let a negative event in your life upset you to the point of disproportionately and inappropriately lashing out at someone else at the slightest provocation. The researchers describe the results of their research in a paper titled "Chewing on It Can Chew You Up: Effects of Rumination Triggered Displaced Aggression":

> In all three studies, provoked participants who were induced to ruminate displayed more displaced aggression after a mildly annoying triggering event than did those who did not ruminate. Rumination appears to augment triggered displaced aggression by maintaining an aggressive internal state. A provocation, such as an insult, increases negative affect and primes aggression-related thoughts, feelings, and behavior tendencies. . . . Thus, a mildly annoying event is perceived as highly aversive and deserving of an aggressive response. If provocation-induced negative affect, however, is allowed to dissipate, the subsequent mildly annoying event is perceived as trivial and is easily dismissed.

Piling on More Pain and Risk

RUMINATION DOES NOT PAY, AND ULTIMATELY, IT BRINGS US MORE PAIN.

We suffer an original offense again and again when we give it undue attention and exaggerate its importance in our lives. Ruminating about the offense and our desire for revenge only assures us of continued frustration, anger, and disappointment. Bushman and his colleagues conclude:

> How individuals focus their attention after a provocation affects how they will behave toward others. If individuals choose to focus on their bad mood and the provocation that elicited it, they may unfairly lash out against innocent others. If, instead, they choose to let their negative mood dissipate and focus on other events, they are less likely to lash out.

When you center your life on revenge and ruminate about every provocation and slight, you jeopardize everyone's health, safety, and happiness—including your own.

When you don't let Garbage Trucks pass you by, you put others at risk, as well as yourself.

Your Action Guide

Some people try to get even with people. Others spend their energy fantasizing about revenge.

How about you? How have Garbage Trucks stolen your happiness and success? Write your answer below.

Commit to this goal: Reject revenge and offer forgiveness instead. Then, write below how you feel about yourself and your relationship with the people around you.

CHAPTER TEN

Real-time Forgiveness

Forgiveness is not an occasional act: It is an attitude.
—Martin Luther King, Jr.

I WOKE UP EARLY TO CATCH A 7:00 A.M. FLIGHT. I WAS TIRED FROM STAYING UP late the previous night to prepare for a series of meetings the next day.

I was working for Yahoo! at the time. We had just bought another company, and I was traveling to San Diego to help evaluate its operations. I was anxious because I knew I would have to recommend that we cut positions.

At the airport, I met two of my colleagues and bought each of us a cup of coffee. When we boarded the plane, I set my coffee down as I placed my briefcase in the overhead compartment.

The flight was a little choppy but nothing out of the ordinary, and my coworkers and I spent a good part of it reviewing the day's plan. When we pulled into the gate, people started scrambling for position to get out, as they invariably do on every flight. Just then a man started yelling and swearing. "Who did this?! Who the #@!© did this?!" I looked around and saw a big man in the aisle. People were backing away from him.

He yelled, "Who the #©!@ spilled coffee all over my jacket?" A jolt of electricity went through me. I frantically looked around. Where was my coffee? I couldn't find it. I looked back. The guy was still yelling, only now he was holding his coat and an empty cup. Right then, I knew it was me. I'd forgotten about my coffee. I was the guy he was looking for. When I put my bag in the overhead compartment, I must have put my coffee down in the bin and it tipped over and spilled all over the man's coat. I was mortified and embarrassed; I felt horrible. I also knew I had to own up.

"Sir, I'm so sorry," I said standing up. "I just realized it was me." I paused. "I am so sorry."

The man stepped toward me. His face was bright red and he looked like he was going to punch me. "You're a @!©# idiot!" he yelled. He was holding his suit jacket, which was dark blue and looked wet.

As fast as I could, I said, "Let me give you money for the dry cleaning. Let me see if we can get it cleaned immediately at the airport or nearby." I reached for my wallet and opened it. I added, "Whatever it costs. I'll buy you a new suit if I need to. It's my mistake."

But the man would have none of it. I had to be punished. As the rest of the passengers started getting off the plane, I could see they were relieved to get away from the raging man—and relieved they weren't me.

"Give me your business card!" he demanded.

"Sure," I said, reaching into my wallet. I grabbed a card and handed it to him.

"I'm going to report you to your CEO. I'm going to report you to your Board. Just you wait!"

He then brushed past me, yelled another obscenity, and got off the plane.

Let me set something straight about this story. I was wrong. The man was justified in being upset. He was undoubtedly going to a meeting, and his coat was soaked with coffee. I was a Garbage Truck in his life. I'd made a mistake, I was sorry, and I offered to correct what I had done. It was the only right way for me to respond. His reaction, on the other hand, was not up to me. It was his decision.

Another Story

ONE DAY I WAS DRIVING TO THE OFFICE ON HIGHWAY 85 IN ATLANTA. TRAFFIC was slow that day, but I didn't mind. I was enjoying the drive in my new car on a beautiful day.

But as I was driving, I spotted an animal (it looked like a raccoon) lying in the lane to my left. The driver in the car next to me was looking off into the distance while his car was on track to run over the animal. I was afraid the car might swerve to get out of the way at the last minute, so I quickly hit the accelerator to give the car room to maneuver.

There was a problem, however. Traffic had stopped at the same time and a wall of cars was waiting for me. I slammed on the brakes, skidded, and slid right into the back of another car.

Things quickly got worse. The impact from the collision caused the car in front of me to skid into the car in front of it. Not good.

All three of us pulled over. As we got out of our cars, I immediately checked on the person in front of me. She was fine. We hadn't been going very fast because of the slow traffic. We checked her car and found a small scratch on the bumper. Then the driver of the other car came over to us. He was also fine, and his bumper had only a minor scratch. He introduced himself. He was an off-duty police officer—definitely not good. He asked what happened and I explained what I'd been doing. I told him it was my fault.

The officer nodded and turned to the other driver.

"You are also at fault. You shouldn't have hit me. You were driving too close."

Then the officer smiled, shook his head, and looked at both of us. "We're all fine," he said. "There's no damage. Let's forget about it." Then he slapped me on the back and said, "A little more careful next time." He looked at the woman and said, "Not so close next time."

When the officer stepped away, I looked at the other driver, who motioned a sign of relief.

"Yeah," I said. "He was cool."

"Yes, he was," she said.

"And so were you. Thanks," I said. "Again, I'm sorry."

"No problem," she said. "Take care."

She got back into her car and drove away.

Choosing Your Reaction

IN THAT LAST SCENARIO, I WAS LUCKY. THE WOMAN AND THE OFFICER could have acted differently. Whatever my excuse, I still caused an accident—I'd been a Garbage Truck in both of their lives, and they were justified to be angry. But they weren't. They had the right to lash out at me.

But they didn't. They chose to forgive me, and they left the scene better than when they'd entered it.

In both of these stories, I was at fault. Although I have not bumped a car or spilled coffee on someone's jacket since then, I've made other mistakes. And each time I was in error, someone else had to react. How they responded was their choice.

I've also been on the receiving end of other people's mistakes. I could not—in most cases—control their errors. I could only control my responses. How did I want to react? How did I want to address the situations? How did I want to leave the experiences? Did I want to judge people harshly and make them pay, or did I want to offer my understanding and let them pass by?

Harsh Judgment

HOW MANY TIMES IN YOUR LIFE HAVE YOU FELT UNFAIRLY JUDGED? YOU DID something wrong, but you felt it was blown out of proportion. Your mistake damned you to a judgment that you were a bad person. You were viewed as insensitive, uncaring, and unkind. Although you regretted whatever you had done, you felt violated because the judgment seemed so unbalanced. Your good intentions, your kind heart, and your normally good behavior were not given consideration.

When other people do not let your small infractions pass them by, and instead decide that you are a terrible person, it's natural to feel abused, as if you've been dumped on.

Real-time Forgiveness

WE DUMP ON OTHERS WHEN WE CONDEMN THEM FOR THEIR FLEETING mistakes, rather than display what I call "real-time forgiveness" and let their infractions pass by.

Psychologist Fred Luskin of the Stanford University Forgiveness Project writes about the power of forgiveness in his book *Forgive for Love*. Luskin found that when people learn to be more forgiving in their lives, their happiness and health increase:

(1) People who are more forgiving report fewer health problems, (2) People who blame other people for their troubles have a higher incidence of illnesses such as cardiovascular disease and cancer, (3) People who harbor resentment and refuse to forgive show negative changes in blood pressure, muscle tension, and immune response, (4) People who imagine forgiving their offender note immediate improvement in their cardiovascular, muscular, and nervous systems, (5) People who learn to forgive report less stress and fewer physical symptoms of stress.

We are given a choice every day in the way we respond to each other. When people sincerely apologize, show remorse, and attempt to make amends, we have the opportunity to show grace and forgive them. We may still hold them accountable and accept compensation, but we can forgive them.

Psychologist Everett Worthington, another leader in the field of forgiveness research, writes about the need to practice the skill of forgiveness in his book *Forgiveness and Reconciliation*: "People need to be willing to employ these skills when new transgressions beset them."

Sonja Lyubomirsky, in her book *The How of Happiness*, advises, "Appreciate being forgiven. Before you are able to forgive another person, a good first exercise is to appreciate an instance of when you yourself have been forgiven."

Life is not a series of discreet events—it's fluid. How you conclude one interaction affects how you respond to the next. How you treat one person carries over to the next person, and that person will more often than not carry that energy to the people he or she encounters. When you forgive people their transgressions, you set in motion a wave of good feelings. When you punish them with your words and behavior, you set in motion a wave of ill feelings.

In his book *Spiritual Evolution*, Harvard psychologist George Vaillant concludes, "The experience of forgiveness when it occurs is not just the notion of being relieved of a burden, but also a joyful eureka sense of having solved a problem. Suddenly, the fight-or-flight response of vengeance is replaced by the calming vision of green pastures and still waters of peace."

In life you can respond either like the off-duty police officer and the woman with a scratch on her bumper, or like the businessman with coffee spilled on his jacket.

You get to choose. Will you offer real-time forgiveness or will you hold on to your anger and judge people harshly?

It's up to you.

A Final Note

AS I WAS COMPLETING THE EDITING OF THIS BOOK IN A CAFÉ, A MAN dropped a large cup of coffee on the floor as he got up from his table. The coffee splashed all over the pants and briefcase of a businessman sitting next to him.

Startled, the businessman stood up. His pant legs were wet and his briefcase was dripping coffee.

The man who spilled the coffee started to apologize. His face was flushed.

The businessman smiled and said, "At least I like the smell of coffee!"

Both men laughed.

Then they each grabbed some napkins and started wiping up the mess.

Your Action Guide

Think of the people you may have judged too harshly in recent months for acting like Garbage Trucks. How did you turn their mistakes into major offenses? Consider what role you played in the incidents.

In retrospect, write below how you could have offered real-time forgiveness to these people and let their actions pass by.

CHAPTER ELEVEN

Ask for Help Without Becoming a Garbage Truck

The mature person . . . makes sure that his own conduct is correct and seeks nothing from others; thus he is never disappointed. He has no complaints against heaven and no blame toward other people.

—Tzu-Ssu

I WAS EMPLOYEE NUMBER 450 IN 1998 WHEN YAHOO! HIRED ME AS THEIR FIRST director of Customer Care. "Do you Yahoo!?" was the phrase of the day, matched only by the sound of the Yahoo! yodel: "Yahoo-oo!" The company's growth was phenomenal, and thousands of new customers were coming to Yahoo! every day. There were nearly 40 million Yahoo! users when I joined and more than 200 million when I left five years later. Yahoo! was the place to be and I knew it. I was grateful. And there was one big challenge: How would we support all those customers?

The Mission

YAHOO! WAS LAUNCHING NEW PRODUCTS, SERVICES, AND FEATURES EVERY week, yet we had only a handful of employees who were working in customer service and almost no customer support infrastructure. We had a lot to do in a short period of time. The question was where to begin.

At the time, we didn't have a system to route incoming telephone calls or a reliable system for distributing, tracking, and answering e-mail. In fact, no dependable commercial e-mail system had yet been introduced that could handle the volume of inquiries from the millions of customers we served. Yahoo! was acquiring more companies, too, which required that we support new services, bring on new customers, and integrate new employees. If we were to catch up and keep pace with customer demand, we would have to hire aggressively, but the available labor pool was small because of the booming Internet economy. To top it off, Yahoo!'s budgets were tight because we were so diligent about keeping costs down to meet Wall Street's growing expectations.

I quickly learned that we in Customer Care were not alone; all of Yahoo! was moving at top speed. Everyone was working hard. The parking lot was loaded with cars deep into the night, and pulling an all-nighter was not uncommon.

Our mission at Yahoo! was compelling—to be the number one place to "find anything, connect with anyone, and buy anything." Our jobs were rewarding, and we had the privilege of working with some of the best minds in the Internet and media industries. Yahoo! was a great place to be and we were all happy to be there, but there never seemed to be enough time for anything. We were constantly putting out fires, rushing to catch up, and planning for growth. And much of what we were doing had never been done before.

More Was Needed

IT WAS CLEAR TO ME IN THE FIRST FEW WEEKS HOW MUCH HELP WE WOULD need from the rest of the company. It was also evident that writing escalation reports, e-mailing, and calling our engineers, producers, lawyers, and marketers would not be enough to get the support we required. If we wanted to get the help we needed from these departments, we would have to be considered an extension of their teams to better influence service priorities. And to make that happen, we had to overcome two problems.

First, we couldn't just demand support from everyone; we had to attract it. No matter how critical our mission was to serve our customers, we could not expect that our engineers, producers, marketers, and lawyers would stop everything every time we reported a problem. Anyone who has worked in a small, overstretched organization knows that there are always competing priorities. For every hour you spend addressing one customer's problem, you lose an hour in developing a new feature that could help thousands—or eventually in Yahoo!'s case, millions—of customers.

Second, customer service organizations are often underappreciated in companies. They're not always considered cool departments to work in. Most people want to go directly into marketing, sales, engineering, and product development, and see customer service as a place to start, at best—not a place to stay. We had to change that perception. We needed to hire the best people to support our complex suite of products, and we needed to retain them so we could build an organization that could grow as rapidly as Yahoo! was expanding.

I also knew that taking on the frustration of our customers—and it could be intense at times—and dumping it on everyone we worked with would not help anyone. We couldn't be Garbage Trucks. We didn't want people to avoid us because we were the bad news department. People had enough stress. We needed to bring relief.

We also needed to be more positive, joyful, and fun. We had to show our enthusiasm for our work and our gratitude for the support of others. We had to project positive energy to the people we were recruiting to join us, and we had to make them feel included and valued. We had to stay focused on making Customer Care a great place to be, and letting what we could not control pass by. We needed a No Garbage Trucks! approach to asking for help.

University of North Carolina at Chapel Hill psychologist Barbara Fredrickson confirms how important positive emotions are to successful business relationships. In her book *Positivity*, Fredrickson writes,

First and foremost, your positivity is energizing to those around you. It's a large measure of what makes you attractive. Also, it's contagious. When you share your own joy, it ignites joy in others, a process that can forge lasting social ties. The more you open up and share your heartfelt positivity with others, the stronger your connections to others become.

The *Five Fs*

SECURING THE ATTENTION AND RESPECT OF THE OTHER DEPARTMENTS IN
Yahoo!, and recruiting and retaining great employees were the two keys
to our planned success. We had to find a way to do both. So we started
by focusing on our values. If we were clear about what we stood for, all
the required staffing, training, technology, and service program decisions
would be made easier. Our strategies and tactics would be grounded in
the type of organization we were committed to building.

While we wanted to be valued, we would focus on being valuable, and
while we wanted to be appreciated, we would focus on being appreciative.
So we launched the *Five Fs* of Customer Care: We were *Friendly*, *Fast*,
Focused, *Fired-Up*, and *Fun!*

Our *Five Fs* message was always the same: (1) We were *friendly* to our
customers, to each other, and to everyone else at Yahoo!. People wanted
to work with us; (2) We were *fast* at resolving customer problems and
internal issues. Our team was quick and responsive; (3) We were *focused*
on our priorities and committed to resolving Yahoo! customer issues; (4)
We were *fired-up* and had plenty of energy to give our best every day.
We'd work all night if we needed to meet a challenge; (5) We were *fun!*
People liked working with us because we made the work environment
enjoyable.

Then there was our *Bonus F*, for *Flexible*. We made sure everyone knew
we were *flexible* and capable of responding to whatever Yahoo! needed us
to do. We welcomed the opportunity to support new products and services.
It was important that we be a No Garbage Trucks! Customer Care team.

Bill George, former CEO of Medtronic, talks about the importance of
having clearly understood values in an organization. In his book *Authentic
Leadership,* he writes, "Values have to be discussed at every opportunity,
constantly reinforced, and consistently reflected in the actions of
management at all levels."

Everyone we hired learned the *Five Fs*. We reviewed them every time
we gave a tour of our customer service operations, and when we spoke
during Yahoo!'s new-hire orientation program.

Our *Five Fs* were a guide for what we said and did. Of course there were plenty of days when we didn't meet our own expectations, but the focus on our *Five F* values made sure our backsliding didn't last long.

The good news was that our Customer Care representatives excelled and were embraced as important internal partners. We were not sidelined—we were a strategic part of the Yahoo! team. In fact, our staff was invited to participate in Yahoo! product-planning processes. Our representatives delivered internal presentations about the service they provided to customers, and they gave what we called "3-Hour Tours" to our executives—themed after the 1960s television show "Gilligan's Island"—and "44-Minute Customer Care Tours" to the engineers, marketers, producers, and lawyers who supported our services.

Over time, we retained nearly all of our employees, and elevated almost all of them into roles of increased responsibility—and more than forty of the employees we hired were promoted into other departments.

The bottom line was that we needed help, we asked for it, and we got it—and we did our best not to act like Garbage Trucks.

Your Action Guide

Think about the times you have asked for help but didn't receive it. Who are the people who haven't been helping you or supporting you enough? Write their initials below.

Now, think about the way you've asked for help. How might you be acting like a Garbage Truck without realizing it? Identify one or two ways you can ask for help—and get it—without acting like a Garbage Truck.

Remember, just because you "deserve" help doesn't mean you'll get it. You need to recruit people to support you. Notice, and then write below how not being a Garbage Truck improves your ability to get help when you need it.

CHAPTER TWELVE

Don't Label Everyone a Garbage Truck

I think we have to own the fears that we have of each other,
and then, in some practical way, some daily way, figure out how
to see people differently than the way we were brought up to.

—Alice Walker

MY INTERNSHIP WITH A SMALL VENTURE CAPITALIST SERVICES FIRM BROUGHT me to West Berlin in 1987 when the Berlin Wall was still in place. The office was located on Friedrichstrasse, an old street at the edge of the city, which at that time felt like a walled fortress in the middle of East Germany. The office was easy to find for two reasons. It was near the end of a subway line, and you could see the Berlin Wall from our windows.

Life in West Berlin was fascinating. Every day I was surrounded by East Germans—sworn "enemies of the West." Led by the former Soviet Union and a member of the communist bloc of Eastern European countries, East Germans were feared by most Westerners. Communists were dangerous and had to be contained at all costs. In short, they were thought to be what I would call permanent Garbage Trucks.

East Berlin

WHEN MY STAY IN WEST BERLIN WAS NEARING AN END, I DECIDED I WOULD visit East Berlin to see what was on the other side of the Wall and meet ordinary East Germans.

In those days you could apply for a one-day visa to visit the city. Staying overnight was strictly forbidden, and I was warned by my colleagues not to break the law in a Soviet-bloc country.

So, one day I secured a visa, went to the border, and crossed over into East Berlin. Every once in a while I would stop to ask for directions. Luckily, one of the people I stopped was a young East German named Stephan, who, much to my astonishment, volunteered to accompany me around East Berlin. Since he didn't look like one of the secret service agents I'd seen in so many Cold War spy movies, I said, "Sure. *Danke schön*." And off we went.

Later in the day, after a tour of public plazas and stores, Stephan took me to a bar to have a couple pints of East German beer—made by the government, of course. (And I can tell you with certainty that this was one thing the government would have been better off leaving alone.)

Since I had plenty of cash to spend—the authorities made you convert $30 into East German marks at the border and you had to spend them all before you left the country—I looked at all the cash in my pocket and yelled, after beer number two, *"Diese Runde geht auf mich,"* which means something like "This round's on me!"—to which the whole bar roared the cheer, *"Prost Amerikaner!"*

After Stephan helped me settle up with the bartender, he asked me if I'd like to have dinner at his apartment with his fiancée. I said sure, and we hopped a trolley and wound all around town, finally getting to his stop. And then something took my breath away.

When we stepped off the trolley, I looked up at the street sign. I couldn't believe it. It was Friedrichstrasse—the same street I worked on every single day. How could it be the same street?

But then, sure enough I looked to the right and there was the Berlin Wall. My office was just on the other side. I remember thinking that on a good day—and I admit it would have to be a very good day—I could practically hit a baseball from my office to Stephan's apartment.

We had a great meal and talked about the two worlds we each lived in—what young people did and what they thought about—and we debated who had it right—the East Germans and the Soviets, or the United States and the West. Not surprisingly, we differed on a lot of things, but we agreed on more things in life than I had imagined we would.

The evening, which had been such a revelation and a pleasure, came to an abrupt end with Stephan yelling, "We have to go! You have to cross the border in forty-five minutes." With ten minutes to spare, we made it to the border crossing.

Walls

STEPHAN'S WORLD AND MINE WERE JUST FOUR-AND-A-HALF BLOCKS APART. Each morning he and I walked on the same street. But even though we had so much in common, we were kept separate by a heavily protected, tightly guarded wall.

Here's what I learned. First, I could no longer write off all East Germans as "the enemy." Second, the Berlin Wall was not the only wall in my life; I had others. In fact, I had built some of them—other walls that kept me separated from people. Of course none of them was as dramatic as the Berlin Wall, but they existed.

The Wall became my reminder to stay committed to keeping communication open in my life. No country is completely made up of Garbage Trucks. As Gandhi said:

> It is quite proper to resist and attack a system, but to resist and attack its author is tantamount to resisting and attacking oneself. For we are all tarred with the same brush and are children of one and the same Creator, and as such the divine powers within us are infinite. To slight a single human being is to slight those divine powers, and thus to harm not only that being, but with him, the whole world.

Bridges, Not Walls

IN THEIR BOOK *WHY GOOD THINGS HAPPEN TO GOOD PEOPLE*, PSYCHOLOGIST Stephen Post and Jill Neimark suggest how we can tear down the artificial walls that divide us. The authors suggest five ways to increase respect and tolerance:

1. *Cultivate tolerance by traveling. Travel to other countries, to other parts of your city, to other cultures in your own environs. When you travel to foreign countries, immerse yourself in the ways of that culture, from cuisine to fashion to politics.*

2. *Increase tolerance by seeking out difference. Find friends of different nationalities and share each other's different worlds.*

3. *Practice tolerance by learning about other cultures. Watch foreign movies and documentaries about other places and cultures. Learn a new language. Attend a religious or cultural ceremony that is new to you.*

4. *Join in a project with others. Try adapting Adam Seligman's innovative exercises from the Tolerance Project. Create a community project to build or repair something with those of a religion, culture, or style vastly different from your own.*

5. *Help those from other walks of life. Take a few hours a month to volunteer to help those who are handicapped or impaired, mentally or physically. As you help them, try to open your heart to their humanity, not their disability.*

Since my visit to East Berlin, I have asked myself, where are the walls in my life? Why are they there? How are they limiting my life? How are they getting in the way of my doing what I'm most passionate about? Who am I labeling a Garbage Truck before I get to know him or her? Are there entire groups I'm avoiding because I've labeled all of them Garbage Trucks?

How about you?

Your Action Guide

Think about the people you don't really know but have judged as permanent Garbage Trucks. You may have listened to what others have said about them, or you may have judged them based on your observation of a single incident.

Who could you get to know better? Choose two people and find out more about them. Write below what you learn.

CHAPTER THIRTEEN

Don't Bait Others

Men more quickly learn and more gladly recall
what they deride than what they approve and esteem.

—Horace

IT IS EASY TO BE BAITED BY OTHER PEOPLE INTO BECOMING A GARBAGE TRUCK.
People constantly complain and criticize, and whether they're
conscious of it or not, they ask us to join the negative ride with them.
The trick is that it's all too easy to take the bait, which helps explain why
it happens so often. The examples below are not extraordinary, but they
represent the types of conversations we have every day. And in these
instances, you'll see that I was doing the baiting.

Business

WHEN I WAS GROWING UP IN MILWAUKEE, THE LARGEST ELECTRONICS
superstore in the area was a company called American TV. The owner, Len
Mattioli, was famous in Wisconsin. He was known as "Crazy TV Lenny" and
was always yelling in his ads on TV and radio: "Buy a washer, get a bike!
Buy a TV, get a bike!" Mattioli hawked his products at full volume.

One day I said to my father, "This guy is nuts. He's always yelling!"
Dad's reply was, "David, he's a good businessman."

My father was right: He could see that American TV's business was
growing quickly and that Mattioli did more than just yell. Crazy TV Lenny
had found a way to draw people into his store. In fact, Mattioli eventually
opened a chain of fifteen electronics superstores in the Midwest.

Sports

I MET BILL ZITO, NOW A SPORTS AGENT WITH SIXTY PROFESSIONAL ATHLETES on his roster, the summer before we both left Milwaukee for Yale University. One day we were sitting in the upper grandstand at the old County Stadium watching the Brewers play baseball. I was asking him about all the players. Bill knew them because he had been the team's official batboy.

So, I asked him: "What's Cecil Cooper like?"

Bill said: "Excellent guy."

"How about Paul Molitor?"

"Excellent guy."

"And what about Robin Yount?"

"Super-excellent guy."

And this is how the conversation went as I talked to Bill about half the roster. I was surprised that everyone was an "excellent" guy. We've all heard so much in the news about professional ballplayers; I thought at least someone would not be so great. But in Bill's eyes, everyone I asked about was an excellent or a super-excellent guy. He refused to give me any "dirt" on the ballplayers. I didn't know if he had any. I just knew that he loved baseball and the Brewers.

Bill's ability to see the good in players has served him well.

A Lesson Learned

I REMEMBER THESE STORIES BECAUSE THEY ARE WOVEN TOGETHER IN a lesson that has stuck with me over the past two decades: Dad and Bill could easily have taken my bait and joined me in becoming a Garbage Truck. They could have gone along with my needless criticism, or in Bill's case, found someone who was not an "excellent guy." Instead, they kept their focus on what was meaningful and would not allow me to redirect their attention to the negative.

You can make the same choice every day not to engage in unproductive, negative conversations just because someone starts one. You can gracefully redirect the conversation to something more meaningful. In other words, you don't have to be a Garbage Truck to get along.

It's Your Choice

YOU CAN ALSO BE MORE THOUGHTFUL ABOUT CHOOSING WHAT YOU TALK about. Before you launch into a complaint or a criticism, ask, "How is this going to help anyone? What good will it do? Will it improve the situation? Will it make us feel better? Will it strengthen our relationships?" And the next time you catch yourself complaining or criticizing someone, ask yourself, "What am I really learning right now? Are my comments and judgments helping me understand why someone is successful, why a business grows, or how a product sells?"

You are likely to discover that quick criticisms seldom lead you anywhere and that gratuitous complaints close the door on curiosity and creativity for all of us. If you want to improve your life, resist getting baited into becoming a Garbage Truck, and if you're sincere about making the world a better place, don't bait other people.

Your Action Guide

Think about your average day and the typical conversations you have, including small talk.

This week, notice how you bait others into becoming Garbage Trucks by the statements you make and the questions you ask.

In addition, observe when someone—knowingly or unknowingly—attempts to bait you into becoming a Garbage Truck.

As you catch yourself and others baiting each other, respectfully redirect the conversation. Then, return here and write below how you feel and what you've learned.

THE FOURTH COMMITMENT

Do Help the Garbage Trucks You Can

(Help Others Stop Dumping)

SOME PEOPLE SEEM TO BE GARBAGE TRUCKS MOST OF THE TIME, and some of them—unlike bad drivers or rude waiters—play important roles in our lives. They live and work with us; they're our customers, our bosses and neighbors, and sometimes even our relatives and friends. So we must find a way to communicate with them. We must help the most important people in our lives amplify their best and leave their Garbage Truck lives behind.

CHAPTER FOURTEEN

The Garbage Truck Communication Rule

All beauty is loved by those who are able to perceive beauty,
for the perception of beauty is a delight in itself.

—Abu Hamid al-Ghazālī

ALTHOUGH MOST GARBAGE TRUCKS COME IN AND OUT OF OUR LIVES, SOME of us work—and even live—with them. In these situations, you may feel that "just smiling, waving, and wishing them well" is not enough. This is probably especially true of people with whom you spend time every day—your parents, spouse, partner, roommate, in-laws, boss, customers, and colleagues, to name some. You may be feeling trapped and don't know what to do. This is why I wrote The Garbage Truck Communication Rule. It is critical to making the best of your most important relationships.

THE GARBAGE TRUCK COMMUNICATION RULE

People who act like Garbage Trucks allow their anger, frustration, insecurity, and disappointment to drown out most everything good around them.

Fortunately, people do not act like Garbage Trucks all the time. Eventually they'll leave the safety of being a Garbage Truck—if even for a moment. They'll do or say something nice, show concern, or offer their help on some occasion. It's then that you must recognize their best. Let them know the good you see in them. Show them how much you care and how much they mean to you.

When you look for and focus on the good in people, you help them see what is possible in their lives. You give energy to what is right about them. Your love and attention may be what enables them to change.

Catching People at Their Best

WE ALL COLLECT AND DUMP GARBAGE AT SOME POINT. THE PROBLEM IS THAT many people act like Garbage Trucks so much of the time that it's hard to see them as anything else. They are difficult to be around. Many are hard to like. Some are hard to love. It's easy to write them off for their bad attitudes and behaviors. But if these individuals are important to us, we must remember that there is good to be found in most people. We only have to seek and then honor their good qualities. Nelson Mandela made this discovery himself while jailed in South Africa's most notorious prison, Robben Island. Here's how Mandela describes his revelation in his autobiography, *Long Walk to Freedom*:

> *Badenhorst had perhaps been the most callous and barbaric commanding officer we had had on Robben Island. But that day in the office, he had revealed that there was another side to his nature, a side that had been obscured but that still existed. It was a useful reminder that all men, even the most seemingly cold-blooded, have a core of decency, and that if their heart is touched, they are capable of changing.*

Now, we know we cannot connect with all the people who act like Garbage Trucks; most of them come in and out of our lives too quickly. We just have to believe that someone, somewhere, someday will help these people. That's why we always wish them well as we let them pass by.

As for the people we live and work with every day, we must commit to amplifying their best. We have to catch those instances—rare as they may be—when they are not acting like Garbage Trucks, because only then do we have a unique opportunity to communicate with them effectively and profoundly.

Your Action Guide

Part I: Who are the people that act like Garbage Trucks almost all of the time? Can you perceive the good in these people even though they regularly dump garbage?

Imagine following The Garbage Truck Communication Rule when communicating with them. List below some of the ways your relationships will improve as a result.

Part II: Think again about the people you believe are currently Garbage Trucks in your life. Consider your role in these relationships. How would the ideal person act in your place? How do you fit that ideal? How do you fall short?

Now, play a game of what I call, "You First." Write below two ways you could change to help improve your relationships with the people you noted above.

Before we insist that other people change, we must be willing to change ourselves.

CHAPTER FIFTEEN

The Time to Talk to a Garbage Truck

I don't like that man. I must get to know him better.

—Abraham Lincoln

WHEN I WAS IN COLLEGE, I HAD A SUMMER INTERNSHIP WITH PROCTER AND Gamble's paper division. It was my job to make sure the grocery stores on my route were fully stocked with our products—paper towels, toilet paper, and diapers.

Each week, I was charged with finding new ways to increase the sale of our products. Sometimes I would ask for and get more shelf space in the supermarkets. Other times I would ask the store to run a special on our products and put up a big display at the end of an aisle.

Now, the key to my success in each store rested on my ability to build a relationship with the manager. The store managers had to approve all my sales ideas and orders. And while I had a lot to learn as a summer intern, I did a good job servicing my stores. My relationships with all the managers were solid, except for one.

Store #10

ON MY ROUTE, THERE WAS A MANAGER IN STORE #10 WHO WOULD NOT work with me. In fact, he did everything he could to avoid me. For example, the first day I came into his store alone (my trainer had briefly introduced me the week before), he saw me, turned around, and headed for the back of the store. On his way there, I heard him say to his assistant manager, "Tell that kid I'm in a meeting all week." Another day I walked up to him, and before I could say anything, he walked past me pretending he didn't see me. For several weeks, he did the same thing.

Every time I visited the store, I wished that I could avoid him. But it was my responsibility to talk to the manager in every store. It was not an option for me to give up. I knew I could not do my job if I could not find a way to get along with this manager.

Another week passed and I was back in his store. As always, I was anxious about trying to talk to him. But I did what I was supposed to do, and I started looking for him.

We were running a manufacturer's special on paper towels that week. My job was to convince him to put up a display large enough to keep up with the expected demand that our newspaper advertisements would generate. I kept searching for him, aisle by aisle. Then I turned down the paper products aisle—my aisle—and saw him talking to one of his customers. His back was to me, so I stopped at the end of the aisle and waited for him to finish his conversation.

Waiting and Observing

AS I WAITED FOR THE MANAGER, I SAW THAT HE WAS BEING FRIENDLY AND helpful—a side of him I had never seen. Before that moment, I had only known him as a Garbage Truck. Now the manager was taking the time to explain something to his customer about one of our products. It was obvious he was happy to help, and it was clear that he liked our products.

The customer put the product into her cart, said thank you, and continued shopping. That's when I made my approach. Just as he turned around, I was standing right there in front of him.

I said, "I just saw how you talked with that customer. It's clear how much you care about your store. It's obvious you are committed to helping your customers. And I get that you see me as a distraction. I'm just another college kid taking up your time. So here's my promise to you: I will do whatever it takes to help make your job easier and to better take care of your customers. I will crack open boxes, stock shelves, put up displays. Just give me a chance, and I will prove it to you."

The manager did not move during my little speech, and he waited for me to finish. Then he said, "Most of the college kids who come in here don't care about my store, and they don't care about me either. They just want to get a line on their résumé, collect their summer check, and get back to school. But I get it. You say you're different. Fine. Go unpack the paper towels and put up your end display."

A Better Relationship

WHEN THE CHANCE CAME TO TALK TO THIS MANAGER WHEN HE WAS not a Garbage Truck, I took it. I followed The Garbage Truck Communication Rule. I told him what I appreciated about him and that I was committed to working with him. He could see that I was sincere and that my intentions were good.

After our moment in the grocery aisle, I never had to worry about the manager of store #10: We had found a way to work together. In fact, he ordered more from me that summer than most of the other store managers on my route.

More Support

MOST OF US HAVE EXPERIENCED WORKING AND LIVING WITH DIFFICULT people like the manager in store #10. We know all too well how hard it is to improve these relationships. Yet, we must try if they are a critical part of our lives. To help you in this quest, I wrote Chapter 24: Venting Can Help, Dumping Will Hurt; Chapter 25: Your Family No Garbage Trucks! Zone; and Chapter 31: Leading in a No Garbage Trucks! Zone.

I'm committed to helping you enjoy healthy, productive, and caring relationships at work and at home. You deserve peace, support, and love in your life.

Your Action Guide

Think of the coworkers, friends, and family members who are Garbage Trucks most of the time. Choose two of them, and pay particular attention to them this week.

Follow The Garbage Truck Communication Rule and catch them doing something well. Then let them know what you saw, why it mattered, and what you appreciate about them.

Write below how you believe your relationships will improve as a result.

THE LAW OF THE GARBAGE TRUCK QUIZZES

How Much Garbage Do You Accept? How Much Do You Dump?

WHEN I FIRST STARTED TALKING ABOUT THE LAW OF THE GARBAGE TRUCK in my speeches and seminars around the world, I found that most people didn't recognize how much garbage they were accepting in their lives. To help them assess the scope of the problem, I came up with a list of questions:

Do bad drivers frustrate you?

Do rude waiters ruin your meal?

Do difficult bosses throw off your whole day?

As I asked these questions, people began to see how much garbage they were accepting in their lives. They saw the opportunity to reduce their garbage intake and increase their happiness.

Then, I turned their attention to the garbage they might be spreading to others with another series of questions:

When you have a "bad day" at work, do you bring it home?

When you have problems at home, do you bring them to work?

Do you get back at people no matter how small their offense?

Again, when I ran through these questions, people recognized that it's not always the "other guy" who dumps garbage. When we're not mindful, we spread it around.

Over time, I expanded the initial list of questions and developed it into two full-blown quizzes that people could take in just a few minutes.

After people took the quizzes, they immediately saw how much they were accepting and spreading garbage. They had a baseline to use to improve their lives, and ultimately, the lives of all the people around them.

I don't want you to have to wait for one of my seminars to make use of these tools. I want you to have them now.

So, take the quizzes, and see what opportunities you have to improve your life and the lives of the people around you.

Are You a Garbage Accepter?

NOW THAT YOU'VE LEARNED THE FIRST FOUR NO GARBAGE TRUCKS! Commitments, it's a good time to develop greater self-awareness. How much garbage are you accepting? Be honest with yourself. Take the first Law of the Garbage Truck quiz to find out your Garbage Accepting Load (GAL).

Evaluate Where You Are Now

REFER TO THE SCALE BELOW TO INDICATE HOW MUCH OF THE TIME EACH statement is true for you. Answer quickly and honestly. Score yourself as you think you are *now*, not as you think you're *supposed* to be.

4 = Always | 3 = Usually | 2 = Sometimes | 1 = Rarely | 0 = Never

_____ Bad drivers upset me.

_____ Rude waiters ruin my meals.

_____ Bad customer service representatives anger me.

_____ Pushy salespeople irritate me.

_____ Unappreciative and insensitive bosses and colleagues frustrate and distract me.

_____ People who don't hold a door open or don't hold the elevator for me make me mad.

_____ I allow people to bait me into conversations I don't want to have.

_____ When I think of bad events in my past, I replay them over and over again in my mind.

_____ When people give me critical feedback, it shakes my confidence.

_____ My family's probing questions and constant advice get on my nerves.

_____ I get annoyed when people bump into me when I'm walking or hit my chair in a restaurant or knock my umbrella when it's raining.

_____ People who speak loudly on cell phones really get to me.

_____ E-mail spam and telemarketers drive me crazy.

_____ I listen to people's criticism more than I do their positive feedback.

_____ I focus on bad news and dismiss good news.

_____ I worry about what people think of me.

_____ When I say hi to people and they don't respond, I'm sure they have a problem with me.

_____ People who race to take a parking spot or a seat in a café or restaurant infuriate me.

_____ I accept people's negative opinions about people and things—at work, at home, or among strangers—without evaluating or checking them out for myself.

_____ I react negatively and emotionally when I am teased.

_____ I am annoyed by people who state their opinions forcefully.

_____ People's mannerisms get on my nerves.

_____ When I imagine my future, I obsess over the worst-case scenarios.

_____ People who complain bring me down.

_____ I get upset when I have to wait in line.

Calculate Your Garbage Accepting Load (GAL)

ADD YOUR SCORES FROM THE TWENTY-FIVE STATEMENTS. WRITE YOUR TOTAL in the box below.

Your Total GAL Score:

Now, check the key to determine how much garbage you accept in your life.

The Key

Locate your score below to find out how frequently you let Garbage Trucks run over you and dump their garbage—and how often you let them pass by.

A SCORE BETWEEN 55 AND 100 INDICATES THAT YOU ACCEPT A *HEAVY LOAD* of garbage in your life.

Almost every day you are set back by the negative behavior of others and bothered by the things you cannot control. You let too many Garbage Trucks dump on you, and you create too much of your own garbage.

You have an opportunity to radically change your life. When you begin to let more Garbage Trucks pass you by, your happiness and peace of mind will greatly improve.

A SCORE BETWEEN 35 AND 54 INDICATES THAT YOU ACCEPT A *MODERATE Load* of garbage in your life.

Too many Garbage Trucks still have power over you, and you are still burdened by your own self-generated garbage. Your attention is often distracted from what matters. While you are not overwhelmed with garbage, it still plays a big role in your life.

You have an opportunity to increase your happiness and success by letting more Garbage Trucks pass you by.

A SCORE BETWEEN 0 AND 34 INDICATES THAT YOU ACCEPT A *LIGHT LOAD* OF garbage in your life.

Congratulations! You let most Garbage Trucks pass you by in your life, and you don't create a lot of your own garbage.

You are free to focus on what's most important to you. You center your attention on what you really care about.

||||||||||||||||||||||||||||||||||||||||||||||||||||||||||||||||||||||||||||||||||||||||||||||||||||||||||||||||||||||||||||||||||||||

Your Answers

THE KEY IS TO LET THE NEGATIVE THINGS YOU CANNOT CONTROL PASS YOU by, so you can focus on what really matters in your life. The more you free yourself from unnecessary distractions, the happier and more successful you will become.

Time to Act

YOU CAN CREATE MORE OPPORTUNITY TO ENJOY YOUR LIFE WHEN YOU focus your energy on what's good and in your control.

Return to each statement in the quiz. Wherever you answered "always (4)" or "usually (3)" or "sometimes (2)" in the quiz, circle the entire statement. Do this throughout the quiz.

When you've finished, look back at the pages. You now have a visual representation of how many distractions are crowding your attention.

It's hard to see the good in your life when you are constantly circling the bad.

Your New Answers

THE GOAL FOR YOU NOW IS TO REPLACE YOUR CIRCLES OF FRUSTRATION with the freedom that comes with letting more Garbage Trucks pass you by.

Spend time reviewing the first two No Garbage Trucks! Commitments:

1. DO LET GARBAGE TRUCKS PASS YOU BY *(DON'T LET OTHERS DUMP ON YOU)*
2. DO LET YOUR OWN GARBAGE TRUCKS PASS YOU BY *(DON'T DUMP ON YOURSELF)*

Re-read the chapters in these sections and focus on implementing your responses to each chapter's Action Guide questions.

Most importantly, get out in the world and use what you've learned. Your ability to accept less and less garbage will come with practice.

Additionally, make an appointment in your calendar three to six months from today to take this quiz again. Check your progress, and re-commit to lowering your Garbage Accepting score even further.

Remember, this book is for you. Make the most of it.

Your Action Guide

Look at your answers to the "Are You a Garbage Accepter?" quiz and review your total Garbage Accepting Load score. Were your results what you expected? Why, or why not? What did you learn?

Write below what you are going to do differently in your life.

Are You a Garbage Dumper?

NOW IS A GOOD TIME FOR EVEN MORE SELF-REFLECTION: DO YOU DUMP garbage on others? Be honest with yourself. Take the second Law of the Garbage Truck quiz to find out your Garbage Dumping Load (GDL).

Evaluate Where You Are Now

REFER TO THE SCALE BELOW TO INDICATE HOW MUCH OF THE TIME EACH statement is true for you. Answer quickly and honestly. Score yourself as you think you are *now*, not as you think you're *supposed* to be.

4 = Always | 3 = Usually | 2 = Sometimes | 1 = Rarely | 0 = Never

_____ When someone says, "How are you doing?" my first answer is a complaint.

_____ I make excuses for my mistakes.

_____ When I have a bad day at work, I bring it home.

_____ When someone asks me a question, I answer defensively.

_____ I am short-tempered.

_____ When something unfortunate happens to me in my life, that's mostly what I talk about.

_____ When I have an upsetting interaction with one person, the next person I run into suffers the result.

_____ When I'm having a problem at work or at home, my coworkers feel the impact.

_____ People have to wait for me because I'm late.

_____ When something bad happens to other people, I ask for details.

_____ When something good happens to other people, I don't show interest.

_____ I'm slow to apologize, if at all.

_____ I judge people based on stereotypes.

_____ I post mean-spirited—and sometimes anonymous—remarks on the Internet.

_____ I weave in and out of traffic when I'm in a hurry.

_____ I lay on my horn when someone makes a mistake driving.

_____ I make insensitive comments about people of different races, faiths, nationalities, and cultures.

_____ I yell at people.

_____ I expect people to continually forgive me for making the same mistakes.

_____ I spread bad news about people more often than I spread good news.

_____ I repeat the same old negative stories about myself and others.

_____ I criticize people and things more than I show appreciation.

_____ I make sure to get back at people, no matter how small their offense.

_____ I make sarcastic remarks.

_____ When I'm frustrated with people, I talk behind their backs before I give them direct feedback.

Calculate Your Garbage Dumping Load (GDL)

ADD YOUR SCORES FROM THE TWENTY-FIVE STATEMENTS. WRITE YOUR TOTAL in the box below.

Your Total GDL Score: [   ]

Now, check the key to determine how
much garbage you dump in your life.

The Key

LOCATE YOUR SCORE BELOW TO FIND OUT HOW MUCH GARBAGE YOU ARE
spreading to others.

A SCORE BETWEEN 55 AND 100 INDICATES THAT YOU DUMP A *HEAVY LOAD* OF
garbage on others.

You are regularly burdening people with your garbage. The frustration,
disappointment, and anger you carry around with you cause you to act like
a Garbage Truck just about every day, and with everyone.

You have an opportunity to significantly increase your happiness
and to dramatically improve your relationships when you stop spreading
garbage to others.

A SCORE BETWEEN 35 AND 54 INDICATES THAT YOU DUMP A *MODERATE LOAD*
of garbage on others.

You are still disrupting other people's lives unnecessarily—and too
often—with the amount of garbage you're dumping.

Your response to the hassles and upsets in your life often cause you to
become someone else's Garbage Truck.

You have an opportunity to improve your relationships and increase
your own happiness by letting more Garbage Trucks pass you by and by
reducing the garbage you spread to others.

A SCORE BETWEEN 0 AND 34 INDICATES THAT YOU DUMP A *LIGHT LOAD* OF
garbage on others.

Congratulations! You rarely spread garbage to others. Your
relationships are thriving. You focus on what's important in your life, and you
help others to do the same.

||||||||||||||||||||||||||||||||||||||||||||||||||||||||||||||||||||||||||||||||||||||||||||||||||||||||||||||||||||||||||||||||||||||||||||||||||||||||||||||||||||

Your Answers

WHEN YOU REDUCE THE NUMBER OF TIMES YOU RUN PEOPLE OVER AND dump your garbage, you free others to remain focused on what's important in their lives. You are not a Garbage Dumper.

Time to Act

AS YOU DID WHEN REVIEWING THE "ARE YOU A GARBAGE ACCEPTER?" QUIZ, take this opportunity to improve your life and the lives of those around you. Take another look at each statement in the quiz.

Wherever you answered "always (4)" or "usually (3)" or "sometimes (2)," grab a pencil or pen and lightly shade in each statement.

When you've finished shading the statements, look back at the pages. You now have a visual representation of the darkness you bring to others when you act like a Garbage Truck. You can see the opportunity you have to reduce the garbage you dump on others and how much joy you can spread instead.

Your New Answers

THE REALITY IS THAT WE ALL HAVE OUR GARBAGE TRUCK MOMENTS. THE goal is to reduce your garbage dumping as much as possible. Whenever you do, you brighten the lives of others and lighten their garbage load.

Spend time reviewing the third and fourth No Garbage Trucks! Commitments:

3. DO AVOID BECOMING SOMEONE ELSE'S GARBAGE TRUCK (*DON'T LET OTHERS DUMP ON YOU*)
4. DO HELP THE GARBAGE TRUCKS YOU CAN (*HELP OTHERS STOP DUMPING*)

Re-read the chapters in these sections and focus on implementing your responses to each chapter's Action Guide questions.

Most importantly, get out in the world and use what you've learned. Your ability to dump less and less garbage will come with practice.

Additionally, make an appointment in your calendar three to six months from today to take this quiz again. Check your progress, and re-commit to lowering your Garbage Dumping score even further.

Your Action Guide

Look at your answers to the "Are You a Garbage Dumper?" quiz and review your total Garbage Dumping Load score. Were your results what you expected? Why or why not? What did you learn?

Write below what you are going to do differently in your life.

Calculating Your Total Garbage Load

THE KEY TO YOUR PSYCHOLOGICAL AND PHYSICAL HEALTH IS TO LET AS many Garbage Trucks pass you by as possible and to spread as little garbage as possible. When you stop acting like a Garbage Truck yourself, you improve the quality of life for others. But you also improve the quality of your own life, because people respond better to you—with more love. When you receive and spread love, you make the world a better place.

It's now time to see how you're doing. Plot your current Garbage Accepting Load (GAL) and your Garbage Dumping Load (GDL) on the Garbage Truck graph. Remember: The goal is to reduce your Total Garbage Load (TGL). By visualizing your TGL, you may more easily recognize whether or not you have a problem.

Follow the Directions Below:

PLOT YOUR GAL SCORE BY MAKING A DOT ON THE GAL LINE ON THE LEFT SIDE of the garbage truck.

Plot your GDL score by making a dot on the GDL line on the right side of the garbage truck.

Draw a straight line between the two points.

Now color in the space below the line you drew and between the GAL and GDL lines. This shaded area is your Total Garbage Load, a graphic depiction of the total garbage you accept and dump. It represents your opportunity to let more Garbage Trucks pass you by and to spread less garbage to others in the future.

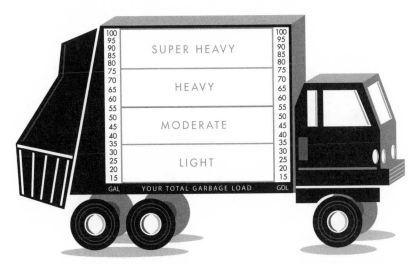

Your Action Guide

What can you do to reduce your Total Garbage Load? How can you let more Garbage Trucks pass you by? Are there other ways you can stop dumping garbage?

Make a list below of three things you will do this week to further reduce your Total Garbage Load.

THE FIFTH COMMITMENT

Do Honor Your No Garbage Trucks! Pledge

EVERYONE LIKES THE FEELING OF KNOWING SOMETHING AND CHECKING IT OFF.

The challenge is that when we know something, we're tempted to stop learning more about it. We stop working on it. We stop practicing. We think we're ready for the next thing, so we drop our guard. And then life has a way of testing us. We learn that we really didn't know what we thought we knew.

This is true of The Law of the Garbage Truck: We need it to be ingrained in us. The use of The Law has to become instinctive. As soon as we recognize Garbage Trucks, we must let them pass by. We need to make a No Garbage Trucks! Pledge, and we need to honor it.

CHAPTER SIXTEEN

I Made My No Garbage Trucks! Pledge

*Waste no more time arguing what
a good man should be. Be one.*

—Marcus Aurelius Antoninus Augustus

ONE MORNING THREE YEARS AGO, A GARBAGE TRUCK RAN OVER ME AT WORK and dumped his garbage. My whole day was thrown off course. I was distracted, moody, and impatient with others. I fell behind in my plans for the day and struggled to make progress on important initiatives. At around 3:10 p.m., it suddenly hit me. I had twenty minutes to make a thirty-minute drive to my older daughter's summer camp. Eliana was four at the time. She was participating in a presentation in front of all the children, counselors, and parents, and I'd promised her I'd be there.

I dropped what I was doing, flew out of the office, and ran to my car. I tore out of the parking lot and drove as fast as I could manage, darting in and out of lanes, leaning on my horn, and rushing through yellow lights. I was frustrated each time someone drove slowly in front of me and when I had to stop for a red light. As I drove, I kept staring at the traffic and looking at my watch. All the while I mumbled, "How could I be late? How could I be late?"

When I finally arrived at the camp, I had to snake around the busy parking lot looking for a spot. When I finally found a space, I leapt out of my car and ran to the auditorium.

Arriving Late

WHEN I ARRIVED, SOMEONE POINTED TO WHERE MY WIFE, DAWN, WAS sitting with my younger daughter, Ariela (age 3). I quickly walked down the aisle to their row. I stepped over and around knees and feet on the way to my seat, blocking everyone's view as I passed. When I finally made it, I sat down and kissed Dawn and Ariela.

I whispered, "I'm sorry."

Dawn smiled.

I leaned back into Dawn and said, "Did I miss anything?"

She said, "Eliana was just brought on stage to recite the opening prayer in front of the whole camp."

I looked down at my watch. I was nine minutes late.

I looked up at Dawn. "Did she see you?" I said.

"She looked right at us and waved."

I dropped my head.

"Nine minutes," I thought to myself. "How could I have missed it? Eliana looked out and saw her mom and sister. I wasn't there, and for what?"

Becoming the Garbage Truck

THE NEXT DAY ON MY DRIVE TO WORK I THOUGHT ABOUT WHAT HAD happened the day before. How could I have missed my daughter's big moment? Then it hit me. I became a Garbage Truck as soon as I let a Garbage Truck run over me. I was a Garbage Truck at work when I was distracted, moody, and impatient with others. I was a Garbage Truck when I left work late and drove aggressively to get to the presentation. I was a Garbage Truck when Dawn and Ariela had to sit alone, and when I stepped in front of other people in the auditorium and surely banged their knees and stepped on their toes. The worst of it was that I missed an opportunity to share a special moment with my daughter.

The truth is that I wasn't there for Eliana because I had taken someone else's garbage and spread it to others, including the people I love the most. I thought I knew all about Garbage Trucks, but somehow I had managed to become one anyway.

But the story doesn't end there.

It's a fact that the Garbage Truck I let dump on me that morning cast a shadow over my whole day—it took my attention away from what mattered most to me, but it wasn't the only reason I was late. I had a history of not being on time.

I had a habit of packing so much into my days that a distraction—or anything else I hadn't planned on—would put me behind schedule. Then, I'd have to rush to make up the time. Although there were many times when I could pull this off, there were plenty of other occasions when I arrived late. My little girl's special presentation was one of them. When I needed to be there for her, I wasn't.

Making My Pledge

I KNEW THEN THAT I HAD TO MAKE A PLEDGE TO MYSELF. I HAD TO STOP accepting garbage in my life, and I had to stop dumping my own garbage. So I pulled my car to the side of the road, reached for a pen, grabbed a piece of paper, and wrote this pledge.

THE NO GARBAGE TRUCKS! PLEDGE

I do not accept garbage in my life.

When I see Garbage Trucks,
I do not take them personally.
I just smile.
I wave.
I wish them well.
And I move on.

And I do not spread garbage to others.
I am not a Garbage Truck!

I do not accept garbage in my life.

I said The Pledge out loud, over and over again. I memorized it and shared it with Dawn. I shared it with my children, parents, friends, and team members. I put a copy in my wallet and planner and on my desk and office wall.

Applying The Pledge

THEN I PUT THE PLEDGE TO WORK IN MY LIFE. WHEN I SAW GARBAGE Trucks coming my way, I would say The Pledge to myself, often in shorthand: "I am not a Garbage Truck" or "I do not take it personally" or "I just smile, wave, wish them well, and I move on."

When I would catch myself in a bad mood at work or at home, I would repeat, "I do not spread garbage to others" or "I am not a Garbage Truck." And when I would find myself slipping back into my habit of rushing, I would say to myself, "I don't want to be a Garbage Truck. I don't want to be late."

When I reframed my life around my No Garbage Trucks! Pledge, it became easier to recognize when I was accepting garbage and when I was dumping it.

Low Drama, High Impact

THE BIRTH OF THE NO GARBAGE TRUCKS! PLEDGE DID NOT COME OUT OF A life-or-death situation or any other dramatic experience for that matter. It was born out of the realization that I was letting other people's negativity degrade my life, and their influence was making me less of a parent, spouse, friend, coworker, boss, and neighbor. And it wasn't just "them." I realized how my habits and decisions were making me a Garbage Truck, too.

When I accepted and dumped garbage, I hurt myself and others. I wrote The Pledge to change that.

Becoming Happier

THE MORE I HONORED MY NO GARBAGE TRUCKS! PLEDGE, THE HAPPIER I became. Every time I let a Garbage Truck pass me by and each time I stopped spreading my own garbage, I achieved greater freedom.

I became free to enjoy every day, free to love and care about the people who matter most to me, and free to focus on what is important in my life.

Your Action Guide

We must always have what I call a "Law of the Garbage Truck Project." We all should be working to reduce the garbage we accept and the garbage we dump.

When we continually strive to improve, we honor our No Garbage Trucks! Pledge.

So, think of your schedule, your habits, and your temperament. When do you typically become a Garbage Truck? What can you change in your thoughts and actions that will lessen the likelihood of you becoming a Garbage Truck?

List below three changes you will make this month: This is your Law of the Garbage Truck Project.

Now, pause for a moment and reflect on what you're doing. Notice how good it feels to be on a mission to change yourself, your relationships, and thereby, change the world.

CHAPTER SEVENTEEN

Taking Your Own No Garbage Trucks! Pledge

What one has, one ought to use; and whatever
he does, he should do with all his might.

—Marcus Tullius Cicero

AFTER I WROTE THE NO GARBAGE TRUCKS! PLEDGE AND IMPLEMENTED IT in my life, I decided I wanted to share it with as many people as possible. Millions of people had already read the essence of my No Garbage Trucks! philosophy in my newspaper columns "The Law of the Garbage Truck" and "Beware of Garbage Trucks!" and on my blog and website, www.thelawofthegarbagetruck.com. And thousands more had seen me share The Law in my live speeches and seminars, and in my short-format television series, "The Happiness Answer."

Living The Pledge

ALTHOUGH PEOPLE WERE LEARNING THE IMPORTANCE OF LETTING GARBAGE Trucks pass them by through my columns, blog, website, newsletters, and seminars, I also knew they might fall into the same trap as I had. Thinking you know The Law of the Garbage Truck is not enough. You have to live it—and you have to make a pledge.

I began sharing The No Garbage Trucks! Pledge with all my clients. I brought it to organizations as diverse as a Florida engineering association, a South Carolina dental association, a Delray Beach inner-city school, a California community bank, an Illinois county government association, and the United States sales force of an Australian-based international logistics company. I shared it with national leaders from more than one hundred countries in AIESEC—the world's largest university-based leadership program—and I shared it with hundreds of people on the streets of New York City when I filmed The Law of the Garbage Truck for my television show.

Making the Commitment

EVERY TIME I SHARE THE PLEDGE, THE RESULTS ARE THE SAME. PEOPLE understand that taking and then honoring The Pledge is the key when beginning to make important changes in their lives.

Now, as I do with all my groups, I am going to ask you to take The No Garbage Trucks! Pledge with me. I believe we learn the most when we're fully involved and having fun. So, I want you to follow along with me as if you were participating in one of my seminars or speeches. Here's the first step. Read The Pledge again now.

THE NO GARBAGE TRUCKS! PLEDGE

I do not accept garbage in my life.

When I see Garbage Trucks,
I do not take them personally.
I just smile.
I wave.
I wish them well.
And I move on.

And I do not spread garbage to others.
I am not a Garbage Truck!

I do not accept garbage in my life.

Now, here's the second step. We're going to say The Pledge out loud together, and we're going to get our bodies into it. This might be the only time while reading this book that you should consider going somewhere private. I don't want you to be self-conscious, and more importantly, I don't want you to get kicked out of your office or home!

Okay, let's do it. Stand up and pretend that you're with me in a big auditorium. I want you to imagine hearing me read a line of The Pledge. And then I want you to repeat the same line out loud. Use your hands and body to emphasize the words.

Ready? Here we go.

David: I do not accept garbage in my life.
You: I do not accept garbage in my life.

David: When I see Garbage Trucks,
You: When I see Garbage Trucks,
David: I do not take them personally.
You: I do not take them personally.
David: I just smile.
You: I just smile.
David: I wave.
You: I wave.
David: I wish them well.
You: I wish them well.
David: And I move on.
You: And I move on.

David: And I do not spread garbage to others.
You: And I do not spread garbage to others.
David: I am not a Garbage Truck!
You: I am not a Garbage Truck!

David: I do not accept garbage in my life.
You: I do not accept garbage in my life.

Congratulations! You have now joined thousands of people who have already taken The No Garbage Trucks! Pledge. Welcome to a life fully focused on what matters most to you.

Your Action Guide

Think of the No Garbage Trucks! Pledge you just made. Write below two things you can do that will help you remember and abide by your pledge.

CHAPTER EIGHTEEN

Your No Garbage Trucks! Pledge at Work

*I don't know what your destiny will be, but one thing I do know:
the only ones among you who will be really happy are
those who have sought and found how to serve.*

—Albert Schweitzer

OVER THE YEARS, I'VE STAYED IN HUNDREDS OF HOTELS AND SEEN firsthand the challenges that hotel personnel encounter on a daily basis—and at every level of the organization. Guests want their vacations and business trips to be flawless. And when they experience disruptions, they can be overly demanding and abusive to the hotel staff: They can become Garbage Trucks.

Given what hotel staff members have to endure at times, I especially appreciate great service when I receive it. Nine years ago, my wife and I experienced service worth talking about.

On the Beach

DAWN AND I WERE CELEBRATING OUR SECOND WEDDING ANNIVERSARY AT the Hyatt Hotel in Kauai, Hawaii. On the second day of the vacation, we decided to go for a swim.

When we finished our dip in the ocean, we went back to our cabana and started to towel off. Suddenly Dawn cried out, "Oh my gosh! Oh my gosh!" She was looking down at her hand. The two-carat diamond in her engagement ring was gone. Two prongs were bent and the other two were missing. I did my best to comfort her.

"We'll get another ring," I said. "It's just a symbol of what we have . . . what we have is each other . . . and that's all that matters."

Don't get me wrong, I really liked that ring—I had searched long and hard for it and had saved up to buy it. But most importantly, it was the diamond I gave to Dawn when I asked her to marry me. Now, it was lost in the sand.

Needing Help

ALTHOUGH I WAS PRETTY SURE DAWN'S DIAMOND WAS GONE FOREVER, I asked Yvette, one of the hotel managers, for help searching for it. To my surprise, Yvette immediately rounded up a small search party. Five of her team members came with her to help us look for the ring. Together we retraced our steps and combed the sand inch by inch around our cabana.

After more than an hour, I called off the search. We had tried our best, but the task was too great. While the ring had sentimental value, I knew the ring was insured. But our vacation wasn't. We needed to put the lost ring behind us.

The Call

FOUR DAYS AFTER WE RETURNED HOME, DAWN RECEIVED A CALL.

"Mrs. Pollay? This is Yvette from the Hyatt in Kauai."

"Hi Yvette. How are you?" Dawn remembered her from the hotel.

"Mrs. Pollay, I have good news."

Yvette paused. Dawn waited.

"We found your diamond!"

"What?!" Dawn jumped out of her chair. "Are you serious?! I can't believe it!"

"We did!" Yvette exclaimed.

"That's incredible!" Dawn said. "How did you find it?!"

"Mrs. Pollay, when you thought we had stopped looking, we kept searching," Yvette explained. "We figured out your schedule. We knew more or less when you came to the beach each day and when you left. So, before you arrived and after you left, we would go out and search. We continued searching after you returned home to California. And this morning we found your diamond."

"Yvette, that's unbelievable. You guys are amazing! Thank you so much."

"Our pleasure, Mrs. Pollay." Yvette was humble but proud of her team's effort and success.

Yvette said, "We had your diamond sent to the jeweler to get it cleaned up, even though the sand actually did a pretty good job."

Dawn and Yvette both laughed.

"Mrs. Pollay, your diamond is now in a pouch, safely wrapped, and on its way back to you."

"Thank you again, Yvette."

Dawn immediately called me at work and told me the whole story.

Service That Matters

DAWN AND I WERE AMAZED AND GRATEFUL. WE HAD NEVER EXPERIENCED OR witnessed such incredible service—and it meant a great deal to us personally that Yvette and her team had gone to such lengths to find something that was clearly precious to us. As a consequence, we felt emotionally connected to Yvette, her team, and the Hyatt.

Did Yvette and her team's extraordinary effort matter to the Hyatt Hotel chain? It did and it does. Here is an important reason why. Because of the great service we experienced, Dawn and I have told this story to hundreds of people in person and to thousands more through my writing, seminars, and speeches. Every time we tell the story, we are promoting Hyatt Hotels. There is no better form of advertising than a personal story we share with others.

When employees offer incredible service, it makes a difference.

The bottom line is that we all have an opportunity to make the world a better place every time we pick up the phone, answer an e-mail, or greet a customer. Who knows how far-reaching the positive impact of our service will be. We cannot be deterred from our mission by the occasional—or even frequent—run-in with a Garbage Truck. We must be ready to make our next service encounter our best. That's what Yvette and her team at the Hyatt did when they looked for and found a diamond in the sand.

Improve Service: Take The Pledge

IN MY EXPERIENCE, ONE OF THE MOST IMPORTANT THINGS A COMPANY CAN do to improve its service is to have everyone learn The Law of the Garbage Truck and take The No Garbage Trucks! Pledge.

When customers are irate, unreasonable, and unfair—and act like Garbage Trucks—it takes a great toll on you. If you haven't learned how to let Garbage Trucks pass you by, you unknowingly take in the negative energy of the customers you serve, and then, inadvertently, you spread your frustration to your next customers.

It gets worse: If your coworkers don't know The Law of the Garbage Truck, they too will become burdened by the negative wave of energy that was originally caused by your responses to difficult customers.

Emotional Labor

WHEN WE LET GARBAGE TRUCKS RUN US OVER, WE EXPERIENCE "EMOTIONAL labor," a term psychologists use to describe the energy and purposeful effort required of people to manage their emotions and keep them in line with the standards of an organization.

In business, the expectation is that we must be friendly, respectful, and courteous at all times, no matter what the circumstances. We often go to training programs designed to outfit us with the skills required to meet this expectation, and our managers are asked to provide us with timely and effective coaching to help us achieve higher levels of performance.

The challenge is that when customers act unreasonably and unfairly, we naturally find it more difficult to properly control our emotions, no matter how much training or coaching we have received. Under this pressure, our "emotional labor" is greatly increased. It becomes easier to get upset and distracted. This, in turn, often reduces the level of service we offer our customers and also negatively impacts our job satisfaction. And, if our training or management support is inadequate, we feel the pain of unreasonable customer behavior even more.

The Power of The Pledge

WHEN WE LET GARBAGE TRUCKS RUN OVER US, IT'S HARD TO OFFER OUR customers the best service. Thus, one of the most important skills you can learn is how to let Garbage Trucks pass you by. The more you are able to focus on resolving your customers' issues without being distracted by their personalities and behaviors, the more likely you will solve their problems.

Imagine how much more enjoyable your job would be if you didn't let difficult customers get under your skin and ruin your day. Your emotional labor would be decreased and your positive energy increased. Work would be more fulfilling, and your customers would be delighted.

When you take The No Garbage Trucks! Pledge and honor it, you are at your best and you can let the negative things you can't control pass you by. What you are left with is more energy to focus on the good in your colleagues, your customers, and your business.

Your Action Guide

How will your business improve when everyone in your organization takes The No Garbage Trucks! Pledge? Make a commitment this week to honor your Pledge in each of your customer interactions. Write below the increased satisfaction you feel and the improved service you are able to provide as a result.

If you lead a business team, make a commitment this month to teach The Law of the Garbage Truck to your team, and have them take The No Garbage Trucks! Pledge.

Provide your team members with timely recognition when you notice that they are letting the negative attitudes and behaviors of their customers pass by so that they can focus on satisfying, and better yet, delighting their customers.

CHAPTER NINETEEN

Your Family Pledge

He is happiest, be he king or peasant, who finds peace in his home.
—Johann Wolfgang von Goethe

I GREW UP IN A NO GARBAGE TRUCKS! FAMILY. I LEARNED EARLY ON THAT "showing disposition," as my mother and grandmother called it, was not permitted. We could talk about anything, but we were not allowed to be temperamental or disrespectful. We could share our problems, but we couldn't take them out on each other. And staying mad was not an option. My grandmother made sure I understood that when I was nine years old.

A Grandmother's Wisdom

IT WAS WINTERTIME IN MILWAUKEE, AND I WAS LEAVING NORTHRIDGE Shopping Mall with my parents, brother, and grandparents after a movie. For some unaccountable reason—I still have no idea why—I was mad at my father, and, in the typical way of so many kids my age, I was pouting and not talking to him.

It was snowing that night and the temperature was below freezing. My father told us to wait inside the mall so that he could warm up the van for us and pull it up to the front entrance of the building.

That's when my grandmother came up to me and said, "I don't know why you're angry with your dad. But your father loves you and you love him. Don't go to bed angry with him. Make sure to kiss and hug him before you go to bed tonight."

Then, she pulled me close to her and said, "Tell him that you love him. You never know when the Lord will take him from you."

I think I stopped breathing when she said that. It never occurred to me that I might lose my father. My grandmother's words have never left me: "You never know when the Lord will take him from you."

The Family Rule

FROM THAT DAY FORWARD, I BECAME CONSCIOUSLY AWARE OF THE family rule. We do not go to bed or go away angry—it is mutually agreed that we have to work through our problems. We might decide to get some sleep, or take a breather before we talk through everything, but we make sure to express our love before leaving the house or saying goodnight.

I believe that one of the most effective ways to help a family focus on love and avoid heartache is to take The No Garbage Trucks! Pledge together. When you take The Pledge, you commit to supporting each other through your challenges and disappointments. You don't have to act out, protest, and shout to gain attention; you simply need to ask for help. In a No Garbage Trucks! family, you can expect everyone to listen, work through disagreements, be supportive of each other's achievements, and help one another in every way possible.

Amplifying the Good

WHEN YOUR FAMILY FOCUSES ON BRINGING OUT THE BEST IN EACH OTHER, celebrates each other's achievements and good news, and fills one another with love, there's little excuse for acting like a Garbage Truck. There's always time for discussion and debate, but none for denigration and disrespect.

When you avoid being a Garbage Truck in your family and invest love and attention instead, your relationships thrive. When you see and appreciate what's unique about each other and what's good about your relationships, you lay the foundation for a beautiful life. And when you cherish the time you have with your loved ones, you are happier.

Your Action Guide

How do you imagine your relationships would improve if your family took The No Garbage Trucks! Pledge together? Write below your answer. Then, make two commitments this week.

1. Declare a new rule in your family: You cannot go to bed or leave the house when acting like a Garbage Truck.

2. Be on the lookout for good news from each of your family members. When the good news arrives, provide timely and enthusiastic recognition.

At the end of the week, write below how good it feels to live in a family that honors its No Garbage Trucks! Pledge.

THE SIXTH COMMITMENT

Do Live in The Gratitude Cycle and Live Free of The Garbage Cycle

THERE IS ENERGY AT WORK IN THIS WORLD. WHETHER YOU BELIEVE ENERGY COMES FROM THE POWER OF GOD, THE MIRACLE OF NATURE, THE FORCES OF EVIL, OR THE ATTENTION OF MAN, IT EXISTS.

When you focus on the good in life, express gratitude, have faith, are kind, show love, and share your optimism with others, you give and receive a certain energy: You live in what I call "The Gratitude Cycle."

When you focus on the bad, act impatiently, harbor grudges, complain often, speak ill of others, and languish in pessimism, you cultivate and feed another kind of energy. A life lived this way is one caught in what I call "The Garbage Cycle."

You can choose where to place your attention in life. You are invited every day to live in The Gratitude Cycle and The Garbage Cycle. There are powerful forces pulling you in both directions. It is up to you to decide which invitation you'll accept.

After twenty years focused on living The Law of the Garbage Truck, I am convinced that happiness and civility are only possible when we live in The Gratitude Cycle and when we stay free of The Garbage Cycle.

CHAPTER TWENTY

The Garbage Cycle of Energy

If misery loves company, misery has company enough.
—Henry David Thoreau

THE GARBAGE CYCLE AND THE GRATITUDE CYCLE PRODUCE, ATTRACT, and require energy.

Every time you become a Garbage Truck, you contribute negative energy—your frustration, impatience, judgment, worry, and anger—to The Garbage Cycle. In turn, The Garbage Cycle burdens you with the garbage of millions of others, and you become connected to their angst and anger.

When you're in The Garbage Cycle, you feel pressured, burdened, and stressed. In his research, psychologist Everett Worthington, author of *Forgiveness and Reconciliation,* writes, "People under stress often feel hostile. This hostility is a generalized floating hostility that is aimed at whoever gets in their target zone. . . . People under stress often are angry and desire to act on that anger by lashing out at the sources of stress."

When you're in The Garbage Cycle, you feel self-righteous and believe that what's wrong with the world lies beyond you. Someone else is at fault. Something else is the problem.

The Garbage Cycle

MY FATHER ONCE TOLD ME OF AN INCIDENT IN HIS LIFE THAT SPEAKS TO THE danger of getting caught up in The Garbage Cycle. It happened in Milwaukee when my brother and I were still boys. While he was driving home from work one evening, he made a bad move on the road and it set off a negative chain of events. At the time, he was just nine blocks from home. Here's how he told the story:

> I was on my way home for dinner, and I was anxious to see you guys. I had just turned north onto Oakland Avenue from Capitol Drive. I was late coming home from the office and in a hurry. And back in those days I was a pretty aggressive driver, so I must have cut off another car when I made my turn because, all of a sudden, I see a guy driving a little car behind me honking his horn, yelling, and waving his fist at me. Suddenly, this guy floors the accelerator, whips around the side of my van, pulls ahead of me, and cuts me off. Then he wildly points to the side of the road, as he jerks his car into a parking spot and slams on the brakes. I follow the guy and pull up behind him.
>
> I'm furious! This guy has something to say . . . fine! Let's hear it!
>
> As I start opening my door to step down from the van, I look up and one of the biggest guys I've ever seen in my life is getting out of that little car. The guy is a monster! He looks like he just came from the gym. He's popping out of a muscle shirt. The guy's sweating, and he's raging.
>
> Then he starts marching toward the van. For the first time in my life, I say to myself, "What am I doing? I'm not going to fight this guy. No way. I'm not getting out of the van. It's not worth it." So I slide back into my seat and slowly close the door.
>
> Then "Samson" reaches my van and starts yelling at me to get out. But I'm not moving. I just look at him through the safety of my locked door and closed window and keep saying, "Sorry about that. I'm really sorry I did that. Hey, you're right. Sorry about that."
>
> Finally, the guy backs down and heads to his little car. I pull back onto the road and drive home with my tail between my legs.

When I asked my dad what made him step back that day, he said with a big laugh, "I didn't want to get hurt! He was huge!" We both laughed, and then he said:

> The reality was that I had made a mistake, and I didn't want to make another. Our driving was bad enough. Another bad move and we could have hurt ourselves and others. We sure didn't need to get into a fistfight. I just didn't want to take it any further. I had two boys and my wife waiting for me to come home. And that was the day—your mom will tell you—that I started to slow down on the road. My macho days were over.

I told my father he gets more credit for being smart enough to back down from a fight than if he had acted like a gladiator. Then he added one more thing:

> Who knows what would happen if all that took place today. In the old days, we might have beaten each other up. Today, I could get shot. Worse yet, innocent passersby could get hurt, too. Believe me, I would never let a situation escalate like that again.

Redirecting Your Energy

INITIALLY, MY FATHER HAD CONTRIBUTED TO THE GARBAGE CYCLE; IT WAS wrong to drive so aggressively and accept the challenge of a duel with the other driver. Thankfully, he also realized that he had to stop The Garbage Cycle he found himself in. He knew that he and the other driver were about to cross a dangerous line, so he backed off, apologized, and moved on.

The key to getting out of The Garbage Cycle is taking responsibility for your actions. When you catch yourself dumping garbage on others, do as my dad did and stop it.

Don't let others draw you into bad thinking and behavior: Recognize when you are being pulled into The Garbage Cycle and then quickly step away.

Your Action Guide

When are you tempted to contribute to The Garbage Cycle? Write below what triggers you the most.

This week, pay attention to your negative triggers and make a conscious effort to avoid feeding The Garbage Cycle. Each time you choose to remain free of The Garbage Cycle, take a moment to congratulate yourself: The garbage stopped with you!

CHAPTER TWENTY-ONE

The Gratitude Cycle of Energy

*Three things in human life are important. The first is to
be kind. The second is to be kind. The third is to be kind.*

—Henry James

FUELED BY HOPE AND KINDNESS, THE GRATITUDE CYCLE IS OPERATING ALL around you. While some people live trapped in The Garbage Cycle, you must choose to live in The Gratitude Cycle.

Every day, consciously immerse yourself in The Gratitude Cycle by looking for the best in others and in yourself. Look for the good in a situation and make the most of it; don't waste time and energy on negative things of little consequence. Instead, save your passion for the challenges that demand your attention.

In The Gratitude Cycle, appreciate what you have and express your thanks. Focus your attention on the positive and let the negative things you can't control wither from inattention.

Let me give you an example of what I mean.

A Trip with My Girls

LAST YEAR, I TOOK MY DAUGHTERS TO A BLOCKBUSTER VIDEO STORE TO RENT *Ratatouille*. We found the movie on the shelf and took it to the counter to pay. Then we waited . . . and we waited.

The salesclerk was handling a customer service issue on the telephone. She signaled with her eyes that she knew that we were there; her message was that she would help us as soon as possible. And so we waited.

I could tell that the customer on the telephone was being difficult and would not let the salesclerk off the phone. Our waiting was putting even more pressure on her because she was the only one working in the store at the time, and customers were lining up behind us.

I turned away from the counter and started talking to my girls about the popcorn we would make when we got home. Just then the salesclerk hung up the telephone and called for us to step forward.

"I apologize for the wait," she said.

"It sounds like you had a tough customer on the line," I said.

"Yeah . . . but that's okay. It's all right."

I handed her the money for the rental. As she put the movie in a bag and handed it to me, I said, "Thanks," and my girls and I walked toward the exit.

Before we reached the door, my little girls started to debate who would get to carry the bag. (If you've been around young children, you know the experience.)

I stopped. I had to break the impasse. When I was just about to tell my girls how we would decide who would get to carry the bag this time, the salesclerk came out from behind the counter and quickly walked over to us. She was carrying a bag in her hand. She leaned down, smiled at my daughters, and said, "I have another bag for you girls. One of you can carry this bag with a new catalogue, and one of you can carry the bag with the movie. You both get to carry a bag. How's that?"

My girls looked at each other, smiled, and said, "Ohhh . . . thank you." The salesclerk gave me a big smile and said, "I have two girls. I know about these things." She walked back to her next customer feeling proud.

I walked my girls to the car feeling grateful.

The Decision

OUR SALESCLERK HAD A CHOICE TO MAKE. SHE COULD EITHER HAVE FED THE Garbage Cycle by spreading the frustration shown by the customer on the phone, or she could have fed The Gratitude Cycle by reaching out to help a fellow parent. Our salesclerk chose to stop the garbage and feed gratitude. She followed The Law of the Garbage Truck. She let a difficult experience with a customer pass her by. She did not take it in and hold on to it. She focused on what she could control. With that decision, our salesclerk made the world a more beautiful place.

Good people like the salesclerk are all around us. The next time you witness people stopping The Garbage Cycle and feeding The Gratitude Cycle, tell them how much you appreciate them.

Spread gratitude, not garbage—you'll be happier and so will everyone around you.

Your Action Guide

Think of your role at home, at work, and in your community. Write below one thing that you can do in each of these roles to contribute to The Gratitude Cycle and avoid The Garbage Cycle.

THE SEVENTH COMMITMENT

Do Declare Your Life a No Garbage Trucks! Zone

THE DAY WILL COME WHEN YOU RECOGNIZE HOW PROFOUNDLY YOUR LIFE has been transformed by living The Law of the Garbage Truck, and you will discover how your actions have benefited the people you care about and the world in which you live.

When at last you feel free of the influence of Garbage Trucks, you have the power to take a stand and declare your life a No Garbage Trucks! Zone. Now you can be confident that your commitment will support you through the good times and the bad.

CHAPTER TWENTY-TWO

Perfection Is Not the Goal

Good actions give strength to ourselves and inspire good action in others.

—Plato

THERE ARE CHALLENGES TO LIVING IN A NO GARBAGE TRUCKS! ZONE. Problems get tossed your way, unexpected situations arise, and what seems easy, logical, and reasonable to do while you're reading this book could seem daunting, complex, and hard to implement when you put the book down and face Garbage Trucks again.

The Seventh Commitment is dedicated to helping you prepare to live a life free of the burden of Garbage Trucks in your own No Garbage Trucks! Zone.

Two Reminders

FIRST, IT'S IMPORTANT TO ACKNOWLEDGE THAT THERE WILL ALWAYS BE Garbage Trucks in your life. You'll continue to meet and interact with people who let their frustration, anger, and disappointment dominate the way they act and communicate with you. Some of these people will come and go and others will stick around, but that's life, and it will be okay. You just have to remember there is no place on earth where human beings are perfect or free of Garbage Trucks. The trick is learning how to wish Garbage Trucks well and navigate around them. Each time you let one pass by without feeling malice and you stay focused on what is important in your life, you pass the test. These tests will always be in your life, but you'll pass them with greater ease as you deepen your commitment to living in a No Garbage Trucks! Zone.

Second—but equally important to acknowledge—is the inevitable fact that you, like the rest of us, will be a Garbage Truck at some point. That's life too. No matter how prepared you may be for responding to tough times and difficult people, you'll still get run over and your reaction will be negative and unproductive. At times like these, it may feel as if you've forgotten everything you've learned about The Law of the Garbage Truck, but of course you haven't. You've just lost focus and suffered a setback—and a setback does not make you a failure.

The key is simply to recognize your mistake: You became a Garbage Truck, accepted someone else's garbage, and spread it to others. Garbage happens! The beauty is you can do something about it—as long as you can stop yourself and don't waste time making excuses. Go to the people you dumped on and apologize. Then ask if they're willing to start over, and then tell them what you planned to say or do before you became a Garbage Truck.

Always remember this mantra, "I will not take out my frustrations, disappointments, and anger on other people; I will not leave them feeling burdened by my garbage. I am not a Garbage Truck."

An Eye on the Goal

NINETEENTH-CENTURY SWISS WRITER GOTTFRIED KELLER WROTE, "WE don't remain good if we don't always strive to become better." Keller didn't say we had to do everything right in life. He just said that we have to "strive to become better." That means we can be good to others and be happy without being perfect. Science affirms this idea.

Psychologists Ed Diener and Robert Biswas-Diener, who teamed up to write *Happiness: Unlocking the Mysteries of Psychological Wealth*, note that what is most important to our happiness and success is where we place our attention, how we interpret events, and which memories we recall. In short, the Dieners' research demonstrates that happy people "look for positives (attention), often think of neutral events as being positive, find growth in adversity (interpretation), and recall more rewarding memories (memory)."

This is what the No Garbage Trucks! Commitments are all about—helping to ensure that your attention, interpretations, and memories are not determined by Garbage Trucks.

Earlier in this book you had an opportunity to take two quizzes—"Are You a Garbage Accepter?" and "Are You a Garbage Dumper?" I hope they gave you a clear snapshot of how much garbage you've been accepting and dumping in your life. The goal of the quizzes is not to help you achieve a perfect score, but to reveal where you can accept and dump less garbage. The outcome of any improvement in this area is, quite simply, more happiness.

Your Action Guide

Once again, remember that improvement is your goal—not perfection.

What can you do to make sure you are always improving your ability to let Garbage Trucks pass you by and to stop spreading garbage to others? List your ideas below.

CHAPTER TWENTY-THREE

Declaring Your Personal No Garbage Trucks! Zone

*It is no use walking anywhere to preach
unless our walking is our preaching.*

—St. Francis of Assisi

KNOWING THAT GARBAGE TRUCKS WILL ALWAYS BE IN YOUR LIFE AND THAT you too may become a Garbage Truck from time to time, you need a strategy that pulls together everything you've learned so far. You need to live in a No Garbage Trucks! Zone.

As you've undoubtedly learned for yourself, there's nothing passive about following The Law of the Garbage Truck, despite the perception of some that letting Garbage Trucks pass you by is more of a *retreat* than an *approach* strategy.

On the contrary, The Law of the Garbage Truck requires that you *engage* with the world, not run from it. After all, you have an obligation in life to care for your loved ones, friends, neighbors—and yourself. This is something you can't do if you are in avoidance mode. Living in a No Garbage Trucks! Zone gives you the freedom to respond to difficult encounters, not avoid them. In short, it's a zip code for a place that frees you from fearing the negative. There, with a smile and a wave, you can let the things that are not important to you simply pass by.

A Source of Strength

THE TRUTH IS, YOU BECOME STRONGER WHEN YOU ABSORB THE GOOD IN the world and let the negative things—all that's bad in the world that you can't control—pass by. Living in a No Garbage Trucks! Zone allows you to live confidently and happily in a challenging world. You can still actively debate ideas with people and wholeheartedly disagree with them without personalizing your difference of opinion. You can persevere for what you care about and work for peace and justice, all without becoming a Garbage Truck.

Of course, a No Garbage Trucks! Zone is not a real place. It's a state of mind and a way for you to be in the world that embodies your commitment to focus on what matters and to lay down the burden of excessive negativity. Remember that you do not have to be distressed by your memories or limited by your dark projections of the future. You are as free to forgive and forgo revenge as you are free to ask for help and give others a second chance.

In a No Garbage Trucks! Zone, you can acknowledge and celebrate the best in others while seeking opportunities to communicate effectively with everyone. Honoring and committing to your No Garbage Trucks! Pledge in mind, body, and spirit ensures that you do not accept or spread garbage. And when you live in The Gratitude Cycle, the investment of your energy in doing what is right—choosing gratitude, not garbage—helps make the world a better place for everyone.

Life Guides

YOUR COMMITMENTS MATTER BECAUSE THEY INFORM HOW YOU WILL react to events and people in your life. The key is making the right commitments.

Some people are committed to getting back at anyone who has crossed them, no matter how insignificant the offense. Others are committed to defending themselves against every perceived threat, no matter how inconsequential. Others still are committed to teaching everyone a lesson whenever they make a mistake, judging people when they do something wrong or enforcing the letter of every rule. If you take this approach to life, you will be triggered by almost any incident that provokes you, to teach your lessons, make your judgments, or enforce your rules.

In their book *Stress, Appraisal, and Coping*, psychology researchers Richard Lazarus and Susan Folkman emphasize the critical role that commitments play in our lives:

> *Commitments are an expression of what is important to people, and they underlie the choices people make. They also contain a vital motivational quality. Commitments affect appraisal by guiding people into or away from situations that threaten, harm, or benefit them.*

Committing to Your Best Life

IF YOU ARE COMMITTED TO ENJOYING YOUR FAMILY WHEN YOU ARE WITH them, you won't let a bad driver, rude waiter, pushy salesperson, or nasty customer service representative put you in a hateful mood. Why would you want to elevate the incivility of these people—or your negative interaction with them—over the enjoyment of happy times with the people you love most? If you allow yourself to be set off by incidents that *don't* matter, you are diverting your attention from the people who *do* matter to you.

When you allow yourself to be threatened by even the most insignificant things in your life that appear to be negative, you invest all of your precious energy in self-defense. Contrary to what you may think, this is a waste of energy when you need to be strong, not weak. The cumulative impact of these negative interactions can be disastrous. If each of your days "is filled with cardiovascular provocations that everyone else responds to as no big deal, life will slowly hammer away at the hearts of the hostile," observes Robert Sapolsky, a professor of biology and neurology at Stanford University, and "an increased risk of cardiovascular disease is no surprise."

When you make a sincere effort to be the best parent, spouse, friend, and coworker possible, you will find it easier to disengage from your previous commitments—whether they were conscious or unconscious—to defend trivialities in your life as though they were major threats.

Walking the Talk

ONE OF MY FAVORITE BIBLICAL PASSAGES IS FROM ECCLESIASTES 5:5:
"Far better that thou shouldest not vow, than that thou shouldest vow
and not pay." This passage has served as a guide in my life. It grounds me
as a writer, teacher, and leader. It says to me that I have a responsibility
to embody the lessons I teach and that I shouldn't promise what I won't
deliver. It tells me I should be an example of what I teach at home, at work,
and in my community. My actions are even more important than my words.

So I must do more than write this book, and you must do more than
read it. Together we must practice what we preach. The people in our
lives—whether they are friends, family, coworkers, or people who are
just passing through—will be comforted by our words, but they will be
persuaded by our actions. Together, we must commit to living in a No
Garbage Trucks! Zone.

Your Action Guide

When and where do you seem to run into the most Garbage Trucks in your life? Is it at work, at home, or on the street?

Stop for a moment and imagine one of these typical encounters. Now, visualize yourself approaching that situation in a No Garbage Trucks! Zone. How will you approach the situation differently and more positively?

Write two ways below.

CHAPTER TWENTY-FOUR

Venting Can Help, Dumping Will Hurt

*Don't flatter yourself that friendship authorizes you to say
disagreeable things to your intimates. The nearer you come into
relation with a person, the more necessary do tact and courtesy become.*
—Oliver Wendell Holmes

WHEN YOU CREATE A NO GARBAGE TRUCKS! ZONE IN YOUR LIFE FOR THE
first time, you may be confronted with situations that make you wonder if
you're dumping garbage or venting. Is there a difference?

Here's the short answer. Venting helps people understand your
problems. Dumping leaves people feeling burdened by your problems.

Venting is productive, even needed sometimes, when it helps you work
through your frustrations. At its core, venting is a request for someone to
bear witness to and acknowledge a challenge you're facing. It's a bid for
other people's understanding and springs from a natural need to want
others to relate to what you're feeling.

The ability to honestly and openly express yourself is fundamental to
all your friendships and love relationships. The basis for this communication
is trust. You trust others to listen to what you are going through without
judgment. It is equally important for others to understand that you are
sharing your concerns, rather than dumping your worries and frustrations
on them. You don't want your friends and loved ones to waste energy
trying to figure out whether they are the real targets of your frustration.

Permission

VENTING IS BASED ON PERMISSION: THE UNDERSTANDING THAT YOU CAN sound off to your friends and loved ones when you need to without being judged. Your friends and family provide a safe haven for you to vent.

However, venting turns into dumping when you do not have permission to unload your complaints, worries, frustrations, and disappointments on someone. If you are committed to your No Garbage Trucks! Pledge and feel the need to vent to someone who may not have given you permission, there is only one thing you can do: Ask for it.

When you say, "May I vent for a moment?" you are being respectful. Your question demonstrates your understanding that other people have their own concerns. If you unload without checking first, the implication is that your concerns are greater than theirs: You're acting as if you have a free pass to interrupt other people's lives with whatever you're thinking about, no matter what's happening to them.

So what should you do when you catch yourself suddenly dumping on someone? The answer is simple: Stop. Ask yourself, do I really need to talk about this? If the answer is yes, ask permission to vent. If you are granted the okay, go ahead and share, but if you don't receive permission, show your respect and find a better time.

Duration

VENTING IS ALSO TIME-SENSITIVE. WHEN YOU ASK SOMEONE PERMISSION to vent, it suggests that there will be an end to what you want to share—you won't go on forever. Once you let it out, your venting is over. You'll listen to feedback and then you'll get back to doing what you have to do—and you'll have a better attitude about it. If you let the people who listen to you know how much you appreciate them—and when you thank them for their support—you'll leave *them* feeling good.

Dumping, on the other hand, seems to have no end. It starts without consent and suggests that there is no likely resolution. You waste people's time and burden them with your garbage.

Dumping is also delivered without concern for how the other person feels. You're too caught up in your own problems to express appreciation for anyone else. If you take your relationships for granted, you will leave people feeling bad.

Starting Poorly

JOHN GOTTMAN, A PSYCHOLOGIST AND RELATIONSHIP RESEARCHER, points to another form of dumping in his book *The Relationship Cure*. He calls it the "harsh startup" in a conversation. This occurs when you want to connect with someone, but you begin "in such a negative, blaming, or critical way, you get just the opposite of what you're after: You drive the person away."

In his research with married couples, Gottman found that "96 percent of the time, you can predict the outcome of a fifteen-minute conversation based on what happens in the first three minutes of that interaction. And if the first three minutes include a lot of negativity, blame, and criticism, the outcome is not going to be very good."

Things get worse when you believe that people won't understand how tough you have it unless you make them feel as bad as you feel. It's not enough for people to listen to you—you have to make them feel your pain. In effect, they have to take on your negative emotions in order for you to be convinced that they adequately understand your unhappiness. Instead of describing what's bothering you and allowing others to advise or comfort you, you don't let up until everyone else is as miserable as you are and you've successfully injected your mood into theirs.

Mind Reading

ANOTHER FORM OF DUMPING HAPPENS WHEN YOU EXPECT OTHER PEOPLE to read your mind. For example, if people don't respond in the way you expected after you've shared some bad news with them, you might withdraw, become angry, or worse yet, believe they don't care. This is an overly dramatic reaction. Although it might be true that others missed an initial opportunity to demonstrate their concern or show excitement for you in the way you would have preferred, all is not lost.

Sometimes people are just preoccupied. You may have begun sharing your story before giving them the opportunity to turn their attention to you.

Sometimes all it takes is for you to say, "May I share something with you that I'm excited about?" Similarly, if you're concerned about something and want people's full attention, you can say, "May I share something I'm a little worried about? Do you have a minute?" Your questions center the attention of the people you care about before you start speaking.

When you give people the opportunity to realize that you have something important that you want them to know, you increase the probability of a satisfying and meaningful conversation. When you release people from the expectation that they should be mind readers, you eliminate frustration and disappointment and avoid becoming a Garbage Truck along the way.

A Caveat About Venting

THERE IS NO QUESTION THAT VENTING CAN BE POSITIVE: EXPRESSING YOUR frustration can help you realize that something in your life is not right and needs to be addressed. Venting can also open an opportunity for you to hear a different perspective and to learn something new. However, if you discover that you are constantly venting to others, you're stuck in the divide between feeling regularly frustrated and taking action to change your situation.

Getting Out of the Divide

THERE ARE TWO IMPORTANT THINGS YOU CAN DO ABOUT EXCESSIVE venting. First, you must determine if you have control over the situation. If you don't, try following The Law of the Garbage Truck and let whatever it is that's bothering you pass by. With daily effort this becomes easier to accomplish. Each time you let it pass by, you invest less emotional energy and you strengthen what psychologist Roy Baumeister calls your "self-regulation muscle."

The idea is that at any given time you have only so much capacity to exhibit self-control. So if you tire yourself out by responding to things that are not important—you let Garbage Trucks run over you and you dump garbage on others—you will have less strength available to handle more important concerns. On the other hand, the more you follow The Law of the Garbage Truck, the more your strength and stamina increase.

In their paper "The Strength Model of Self-Control," Baumeister and fellow psychologists Kathleen Vohs and Dianne Tice write, "Daily exercises in self-control such as . . . altering verbal behavior . . . gradually produce improvements in self-control. . . ." The benefits of increased self-control are many, and they are important. In another paper, "Ego Depletion and Self-Control Failure: An Energy Model of the Self's Executive Function," Baumeister writes:

> People who scored high in self-control reported better outcomes in a broad range of spheres. They had higher grade-point averages in college. They reported fewer eating disorders and alcohol abuse problems. They had less psychopathology and fewer mental health problems across the board. . . . They had better and more stable interpersonal relationships. They had fewer emotional problems and managed their anger better.

Following The Law of the Garbage Truck allows you to center your attention on what matters by letting the negative things you can't control pass by. The more you follow The Law, the greater the positive impact on your life, now and in the future.

Here's the second thing you can do to get out of the frustration divide: If you assess your situation and decide that you can influence it, you have a range of options. For example, consider an issue you may have in the political sphere. Take a break from complaining and do something to address your concerns by making sure you understand the reasons behind a policy or decision that you find particularly infuriating or confusing. Most of us skip this step when we're surveying—and judging—politics, whether it's on a national scale or at work. Try not to let your first emotional reaction take over and move into criticism before you have a real understanding of the issues. If you still feel passionately about your issue, do what you can to respectfully advance your position by calling or writing to your elected representatives, contributing money to or volunteering for an advocacy group, or educating and recruiting others to your cause.

One of the keys to happiness is to believe that your life is meaningful and that you can make a difference. Knowing that you are taking action to support something you care about, instead of perpetually venting about it, will make you feel better and accomplish a lot more.

The Five Responses to Complaining

VENTING SESSIONS CAN TURN INTO BAD-MOUTHING AND GOSSIPING IF you're not vigilant. It's easy to become part of the problem if you resort to the same behaviors that you don't want directed at you.

It's also critical to recognize when you're complaining about people who complain. It's too easy for a "positive" person to complain about a "negative" person. (What's positive about that?) Instead, follow what I call The Five Responses to Complaining:

1. If people's complaints have merit, help them *address their issues*.

2. If their complaints are passing and unimportant, *redirect the conversation* to something constructive.

3. If they insist on complaining, *ask them if they need to vent* for a moment. Just asking this question will slow them down, and the emotion behind their complaining will be partially replaced by the effort of thinking of an answer to your question. It may also help to diffuse some of their negative energy. If they say yes and begin to vent, be a good listener.

4. If people return to vent about the same issue time after time, try *directing them to the source* of their problem.

5. If people become a significantly negative influence in your life, thoughtfully let them know how their complaining is hurting their relationship with you and others. If they do not change their ways, *disassociate yourself from them* as much as possible. Then just smile, wave, and wish them well. You need to move on and so do they.

The bottom line is that venting can help when you do it right, and when you don't vent *all* the time. But dumping is never helpful and should be avoided. You must strive to share what's important in your life without dumping garbage on others.

You owe it to yourself and to others to live in a No Garbage Trucks! Zone.

Your Action Guide

When you feel yourself starting to dump garbage this week, stop. Ask yourself, "Do I really need to share this?" If your answer is yes, ask permission to vent; do not assume that you have it. Later on, write below how your relationships improve when you stop dumping.

CHAPTER TWENTY-FIVE

Your Family No Garbage Trucks! Zone

Two are better than one, because they have a good return
for their work. If one falls down, his friend can help him up.
But pity the man who falls and has no one to help him up!

—Ecclesiastes 4:9–10

ONCE YOU'VE MADE THE COMMITMENT TO YOURSELF TO LIVE IN A NO Garbage Trucks! Zone, you need to reach out, help, and give to others as much as you can. Your spouse, parents, and children should feel they can talk with you about anything, and you with them. If you can't share the best and worst of your life with your family, with whom can you share it? However, you must share the events of your life without becoming a Garbage Truck.

Psychologist John Gottman describes his groundbreaking research findings in his book *Why Marriages Succeed or Fail*. Gottman writes, "We carefully charted the amount of time couples spent fighting versus interacting positively—touching, smiling, paying compliments, laughing, etc. Across the board we found there was a very specific ratio that exists between the amount of positivity and negativity in a stable marriage." The ratio he uncovered in studying hundreds of married couples was 5:1. "As long as there is five times as much positive feeling and interaction between husband and wife as there is negative, we found the marriage was likely to be stable." In fact, in three later studies of married couples, Gottman was able to predict which marriages would eventually fail or succeed. The 5:1 ratio was the predictor. His accuracy was an average of 91 percent.

When you declare that your home is a No Garbage Trucks! Zone, you are setting a clear standard for love and communication. Accepting garbage from each other serves no one, and spreading it hurts everyone.

How to Do It

I'M OFTEN ASKED HOW TO CREATE NO GARBAGE TRUCKS! ZONES IN FAMILIES. The first thing to do is to persuade the ones you love that life is better when you don't act like Garbage Trucks, but it's not the only thing.

Your loved ones have to experience their own transformation. They won't change just because you say they have to—they need to see the light for themselves. The easiest way for your family members to illuminate their own paths is to ask each of them to read this book with a pen in hand. Allow them to explore The No Garbage Trucks! philosophy on their own. Once they recognize how many Garbage Trucks needlessly interrupt their happiness and hurt their relationships, they will be ready to deepen their learning. No one wants to suffer an unnecessary burden. When the people you care about realize that there's a way out from underneath the weight of Garbage Trucks, they will be ready to learn the rest of The No Garbage Trucks! Commitments.

When your family members experience these insights for themselves— particularly after they consider their answers to each of the Action Guide questions in this book—the possibility for your family to live in a No Garbage Trucks! Zone will become a reality.

Sharing the same language also helps families. When you say things such as "Remember The Law" or "You can tell me what happened at work without becoming a Garbage Truck" or "I didn't mean to be a Garbage Truck when I said that" or "Hey, lets back up our trucks . . . this is a No Garbage Trucks! Zone," everyone knows what you mean.

Simply calling out "Garbage Truck" in a lighthearted manner can also be enough to make people pause and consider their behavior. When you think "How am I being a Garbage Truck?" the question interrupts a potentially negative spiral and reinvigorates a healthy dialogue. You can then hit the "restart" button in your conversation and talk about what's important to each of you without the burden of garbage.

With your commitment to living in a No Garbage Trucks! Zone firmly established at home, you can further strengthen your Zone by inviting more people to experience it with you. Reaching out to friends is the natural next step. Your friends trust you to share with them what you believe is in their best interest. When you help them live a life free of the grip of Garbage Trucks, you are truly giving them a gift.

Your Action Guide

Think of the enormous influence your family has on you, and you on them. What would it be like to live and engage with your family in a No Garbage Trucks! Zone?

List below two to three things you could do to help your family live in a No Garbage Trucks! Zone.

CHAPTER TWENTY-SIX

Facing the Hardest Tests in Life

We all carry it within us: supreme strength, the fullness of wisdom,
unquenchable joy. It is never thwarted, and cannot be destroyed.

—Huston Smith

WHEN YOU DON'T ACT LIKE A GARBAGE TRUCK, YOU ARE HAPPIER AND YOU increase civility in the world. When you commit yourself to a life focused on what is good, right, and just, you make the world a better place for all of us. As we've already discussed, your No Garbage Trucks! Pledge gives you the strength to pass the tests that life presents you on a daily basis.

But what happens when one of those life tests is harder than you could ever have imagined?

Will living in a No Garbage Trucks! Zone fail you when you are faced with life's worst problems? When illness, trauma, and death lay their heavy hands on your life, will your No Garbage Trucks! Commitments no longer apply? Will some events in your life—and their aftermath—make your No Garbage Trucks! Pledge less important? And can living in a No Garbage Trucks! Zone still serve you and others during the worst times of your life?

These are difficult and important questions. There is no hiding from real adversity: It will find you, and when it does, you can't just smile, wave, and let it pass you by.

Life after Illness, Life after Death

MILLIONS OF PEOPLE ARE CONFRONTED WITH DISEASE, TRAUMA, AND death every day. Their stories remind us that families face illnesses and suffer losses greater than we could ever imagine. People are burdened with heartache that no one should have to bear. For many, there is no way to completely get over their loss; there is only learning to live with it. Elisabeth Kübler-Ross and David Kessler, coauthors of *On Grief and Grieving,* write, "The time after a significant loss is full of the feelings that we usually have spent a lifetime trying not to feel. Sadness, anger, and emotional pain sit on our doorstep with a deeper range than we have ever felt."

My heart goes out to anyone who has ever lost a loved one. I have always said that nothing in life can be so bad, as long as we can be with the ones we love. But what happens to us when our loved ones are taken from us? And what happens when the people we love have a disease that could end their life?

Brave Hearts

I HAVE COME TO KNOW MANY COURAGEOUS PEOPLE OVER THE YEARS who have borne an unfair share of life's sorrows. They have had every right to be devastated after each loss or diagnosis. Understandably, their initial emotions were anything but positive. They experienced all the usual emotions you'd expect following the death of a loved one, or a diagnosis of a potentially fatal disease. What distinguishes them is that they eventually took control of what was left of their lives. In their own ways, they lived through their heartache and found their path back to peace and happiness. Their examples illustrate the power of living in a No Garbage Trucks! Zone.

It's time to hear one of their stories.

Your Action Guide

Imagine the loss you will face one day. Someone will get sick or pass away. You may become ill. You may have already faced tragedy in your life, or you may be facing it now.

Write below two ways that living in a No Garbage Trucks! Zone could help you cope with your loss.

CHAPTER TWENTY-SEVEN

Kim's Story

When you get into a tight place and everything goes against you,
'til it seems as though you could not hold on a minute longer, never
give up then, for that is just the place and time that the tide will turn.
—Harriet Beecher Stowe

AT 37, KIM GREENBAUM WAS HAPPY. SHE ENJOYED MARRIED LIFE WITH HER husband, Steve, and their two beautiful children—Lauren, who was almost three, and Jordan, who was a few months away from his first birthday. Kim had a great job as the national sales training director for an educational software company, and she was able to work from home, allowing her to be with her children for most of the day.

On January 4, 2005, Kim had her annual checkup and all the usual tests, including a mammogram. Afterward, she waited for the results in the lobby.

The Look

WHEN KIM WAS USHERED BACK INTO THE EXAMINING ROOM, SHE SAW WHAT she calls the face of bad news—"the kind of look that makes the hair on the back of your neck rise," says Kim. The medical staff wanted to do an ultrasound because they had found something in Kim's right breast that did not look right. She started to panic and called Steve to let him know there might be a problem. By the time the doctor came in to look at the ultrasound results, Kim knew that all this attention could not be good. The doctor said that Kim had micro-calcifications over 90 percent of her right breast, and a needle biopsy was immediately scheduled for the following week.

Kim had her needle biopsy. It was extremely painful. Unfortunately, it wasn't conclusive, so Kim had to have a surgical biopsy which revealed the presence of pre-cancerous cells. This is not uncommon for women, but it concerned Kim's doctor. He ordered a lumpectomy.

When Kim arrived home after her appointment, she looked at Jordan, who would celebrate his first birthday in five weeks, and Lauren who had just turned three, and thought, "I'll do whatever is necessary to be here for my children." So Kim went to see a breast cancer specialist in Miami.

Whatever Is Necessary

"IT'S RIDICULOUS WHAT YOU'RE THINKING OF DOING," THE DOCTOR SAID. "The likelihood of you ever getting breast cancer is nil." But Kim was willing to have a mastectomy if it would take away the possibility of the pre-cancerous cells becoming cancerous. The specialist dismissed Kim's concerns, but she wasn't satisfied.

Kim spoke to another well-respected surgeon for his opinion. This time it was agreed that if he found any tissue during the lumpectomy that concerned him, he had Kim's permission to do whatever was necessary, including a mastectomy right then and there. She told him, "Think of me as your wife and care for me as you would her."

On April 27, 2005, Kim met with her surgeon one last time before the lumpectomy. Reaching into her purse, she pulled out a handful of pictures of her children and handed them to him. "This is why you need to take really good care of me," Kim said.

When Kim woke up from her surgery, she was shocked. True, she knew she had given her doctor permission to remove her breast if he found anything that concerned him, but it was still a shock to know that her breast was gone. As she thought of her children, however, she was also grateful . . . "Whatever it takes to be with them."

Moving On

A YEAR LATER KIM WAS ENJOYING HER BEST SUMMER EVER. IT HAD BEEN over a year since her mastectomy. "I was riding high," Kim said. She had never appreciated her family more than she did then, and she felt like she had taken control of her life. The year before she had taken a bold step to ensure her health, and now she couldn't be happier.

The Check-up

ON SEPTEMBER 13, 2006, KIM WENT TO SEE HER DOCTOR FOR HER ANNUAL mammogram. She was relaxed, because, as she told me, "It was going to be a piece of cake. I had taken care of everything the year before." However, there was one thing.

Kim had felt something under her arm prior to the appointment. She knew it couldn't be cancer. How could it be? She'd had her breast tissue removed. And even though she was sure everything was fine, Kim mentioned it anyway during the appointment. The medical staff also thought it was probably nothing, but, as a precaution, they conducted an ultrasound.

Kim lay back down on the table as she had the year before. The ultrasound technician made sure Kim was comfortable and started the procedure. The technician looked at the screen, hesitated, and then looked at Kim.

Kim knew that face. Bad news was back. She had a palpable mass. Two days later, before the surgery, Kim greeted the nurse, anesthesiologist, and doctor with a new set of family pictures.

That Look Again

HOURS LATER, KIM WOKE UP IN THE RECOVERY ROOM. STILL GROGGY FROM the anesthesia, she lightheartedly said, "Doctor, are we going to have to get my husband a new wife?" No one laughed. "I saw that look again," Kim told me. "It was becoming too familiar." Then he said, "We need to do more testing, but it looks like cancer."

One week later, still sore from surgery, Kim was on the floor playing with Jordan in his preschool music class when she received the call. It was her doctor. Kim asked him to hold while she stepped outside. She gave Jordan a graham cracker, sat him on a step, got a pen and a piece of paper, and then sat down next to her son.

The News

KIM HAD INVASIVE BREAST CANCER. DESPITE HER EARLIER MASTECTOMY, cancer was found under her arm in the axillary breast tissue that remained. Another surgery was required and Kim would need daily radiation for seven weeks. When she heard the news, "I was panicked," Kim said. "I was looking at Jordy quietly eating that graham cracker, and I thought, 'Who's going to raise this child?' It sounds a little extreme, but that was my first thought. 'Who is going to love my children?' It was the saddest thing for me to think about—not to see my children grow up."

Kim had to undergo additional surgery to remove lymph nodes. Thankfully, the results were clean. Her life has been full of tests and procedures ever since, but she says, "It could have been a lot worse. It's easy to say, 'Why me? Why me?' For me, the 'Why me?' was, 'Why did I get so lucky to find the cancer this early?'"

Experiencing Negative Emotions

WHAT WORRIED KIM MOST WAS NOT KNOWING IF SHE WOULD BE THERE for her children. However, she always kept her emotions positive when she was around them. They were too young to understand what she was going through, and the last thing Kim wanted to do was expose them to so much worry. But that didn't mean Kim wasn't dealing with negative emotions. There were times when she found herself in the shower "bawling her eyes out." She said, "It's a scary time, and you have to grieve a little. You had this healthy and joyful life, and now you're told that maybe you're not so healthy, and all of a sudden your future seems uncertain. So I would have a really good cry in the steamy shower—it felt so cathartic—and then I would step out of the shower, feel the blast of cold air, and I would say, 'Okay. I'm good. Let's go. I can beat this thing.'"

Laughter

KIM AND STEVE ALSO TRIED TO KEEP THEIR SENSE OF HUMOR DURING THIS time. The alternative was to focus on what was worrisome. They chose laughter. Kim and Steve felt that humor helped them keep everything in perspective.

One night I said to Steve, "I want a pizza. Let's order a pizza."

Steve said, "Kim, we have so much food in the refrigerator. Why do we need to get a pizza?"

I said, "Steve, I have cancer. I want a pizza."

Steve stopped and looked at me and said, "Kim, you just pulled 'the cancer card' . . . . I'll get you a pizza if you want one—I'll go right now!"

Then I said, "Oh no. I can't believe I just did that. I just wasted my cancer card on a pizza. I could have asked you to redo the kitchen or buy me a diamond necklace, but instead I asked for a pizza!"

We laughed and laughed.

Kim and Steve's ability to change gears between positive and negative emotions illustrates what psychologist and bereavement researcher George Bonanno describes in his book *The Other Side of Sadness* as a "switch" from sadness into a more positive state of mind.

Most of us are surprised to learn that we can make this switch. We don't expect to find joy and even laughter within our pain, but when we do, it makes sense, and we feel better, even if temporarily. . . . These positive states do more than propel us out of sadness; they also reconnect us to those around us. Laughter in particular has a contagious effect on other people. . . . Laughter makes other people feel better and pulls them toward us in a new way, rewarding them for having bothered to stay with us through the painful moments.

Positive Relationships

AS UPSET AS KIM WAS WITH THE NEWS AND KNOWLEDGE OF HER CONDITION, she never let it get in the way of building positive relationships with everyone who had a role in her care. She wanted everyone pulling for her and trying to help her in any way possible. Kim's feeling was why would she want to have any unnecessary adversarial relationships in her life when she was trying to focus all her best energy on getting better and caring for her family. Her positive attitude helped make sure she received the best care possible. You have to be an assertive advocate for your health; you serve yourself best when you don't take on the burden of other people's garbage and you don't spread your own. Kim says it this way:

> Anyone diagnosed with cancer will have fear. It comes with the territory. A diagnosis can take weeks, and the fear of the unknown is much worse than dealing with the known. Living in a No Garbage Trucks! Zone is a helpful guide for getting through the difficult times. First, it is a reminder that, yes, there is garbage in our lives that is beyond our control. This is important because cancer patients often feel as if they may have brought this upon themselves (Did I eat the wrong food? Not exercise enough?), and feeling bad about how it happened is not going to help anyone.

> Second, it is a focus for what is important. Yes, cancer is garbage; it is dumped on you without warning and weighs heavily on your life. But with the reminder to look for the great things in our lives, and not focusing on the bad like a Garbage Truck, we give ourselves the opportunity to be happy, even as we deal with something as scary as cancer.

Living in a No Garbage Trucks! Zone keeps you clear of mind. When you are facing the biggest test of your life, you cannot afford to waste your energy on unimportant negative distractions. You must attend to what matters. In Kim's case, while she looked for the positive and was grateful for what was good in her life, she remained vigilant at all times about her health. In fact, had Kim not found and reported the pea-sized lump she felt under her arm, her cancer might have gone undetected.

The Power of Pink

KIM FINISHED HER RADIATION ON JANUARY 11, 2007. TWO WEEKS LATER, ON January 25, she was walking in the Susan G. Komen Race for the Cure.

I remember thinking this is where I need to put my attention. I was still so grateful, so I thought it's time to stop thinking about me, and time to start thinking about other women. Because there are women who have it worse than I do, and there are women who are not going to survive this disease, so I have to do something for all the women who may need help. And so I became involved. I started a letter writing campaign. I talked about my experiences. I raised money for cancer research. Then, I started going to luncheons, and I remember looking around and thinking, these are all very philanthropic older women. But I need to reach my friends and peers, the other young moms, before they are diagnosed with breast cancer.

In a year's time three young moms told me they had breast cancer. They came to me looking for guidance, and I thought this is insane. We have to do something about this. We have to do something to help these women. And so I partnered with Joy Goldman, and within six months we organized an educational awareness event for 400 women. We called it "The Power of Pink." It still amazes me to this day, women who come up to me and say, "You know what? Because of you, I had testing done and they discovered my cancer. Thank you."

Support from Family and Friends

KIM ALSO TEACHES US HOW IMPORTANT IT IS TO RALLY AS MUCH SUPPORT from your family and friends as you can with your positive energy. You want to attract people to your side, not repel them. Even under difficult circumstances, if you can make them feel good about their contribution to your health and happiness, people will continue to invest in their relationship with you. On the other hand, if you constantly bring them down, your coworkers will begin to distance themselves, friends will slowly fade, and family members will eventually tire of your bad mood, attitude, and behavior. Here's Kim's advice:

> You can have the greatest, greatest friends, but after a while, they don't want you dumping on them all the time. They also want to hear about the good things that are going on in your life.

> As concerned as they are for you, they also want to know that you're being a good friend to them. We all have issues. It's not isolated just to someone with cancer. It's easy to see the world through your own filter of "Oh my goodness, I'm dealing with cancer." The reality is that everybody's dealing with something that they feel is very important in their lives. And who is ultimately the judge. Which is worse? There's no competition.

An Example

KIM'S LIFE REMINDS US HOW IMPORTANT IT IS TO LIVE IN A NO GARBAGE Trucks! Zone.

> With my own health situation, I am again "under observation" for a palpable mass. My "cancer garbage" may always be a part of my life. The Law of the Garbage Truck is a message of not allowing fear to overtake my life—even as I wonder what tomorrow will hold. I know that I have amazing people in my life and that I am in great hands medically. By letting go of (most) of the fear and living my life with appreciation for everything I have—my husband, my children, my family, and my friends—I am a happy, grateful, pro-active survivor.

Your Action Guide

Think of Kim's journey with cancer and the presence it has in her life. Her gratitude for all that is good and the happiness she feels does not diminish her vigilance to safeguard her health. While some worry remains, her happiness prevails.

What about your life? Do you have a worry or a concern that may never go away completely? This week, pay attention to the way your concern impacts your mood and behavior. Then write below how it can make you accept and dump garbage.

Make a deliberate effort to acknowledge your worry without letting it turn you into a Garbage Truck. Feel good that you can still be happy without denying the necessary concerns of life.

CHAPTER TWENTY-EIGHT

Loss and Authenticity

Be like the bird that, passing on her flight awhile on boughs too slight, feels
them give away beneath her, and yet sings, knowing that she hath wings.
—Victor Hugo

WHAT WOULD LIFE BE LIKE IF THOSE OF US WHO ARE SUFFERING FELT
free to act out in whatever way we wanted? While we might accept the
special status of being entitled to act like a Garbage Truck ourselves, would
we be willing to grant everyone around us the same freedom? Would we
want our family, friends, coworkers, and strangers dumping their garbage
on us—justified as they might feel?

The belief that we are justified to lash out at the world invites the world
to reciprocate.

The Narrow View

WHEN YOU TAKE A NARROW VIEW OF YOUR LIFE AND FOCUS ON YOUR PAIN,
you feel excused from concerning yourself with others. You say to yourself,
"So what if I become impatient, short-tempered, judgmental, or overly
negative? That's too bad. That's what happens when life sends you a
Garbage Truck too big to handle." When you see the world through this
limited view, however, you don't see how acting like a Garbage Truck hurts
you and how it hurts others.

It is easy to justify your own bad behavior (which is completely
understandable) when your pain is overwhelming—but do you want to live
in a world where people use their personal tragedies as an excuse to act
badly?

Although you might want everyone to overlook, or at least to understand, the times you lash out at others, you cannot dictate their response. It is not up to you to decide how others should respond to your anger and insensitivity. No matter how much you love the people in your life, their reactions to you are of their own choosing. You can't control them. They may follow The Law of the Garbage Truck and charitably let some of your behavior pass by, or they may not. One thing is for sure: People have a threshold for how much garbage they will accept from others. The people in your life will eventually have enough of your bad behavior, no matter how tragic your loss or how deep your pain. You will never be given a free pass to act inconsiderately for the rest of your life.

The Broad View

THE KEY IS TO TAKE A BROADER VIEW OF YOUR LIFE. LOOK AT YOUR relationships. How can you love and appreciate all the people in your life? You would be devastated if you were to lose a loved one, friend, or find out someone has a disease, so why would you make the people you care about suffer while you still have them? The best tribute you can pay to your loved ones who are ailing, or have passed, is to live a life worthy of their spirit. Following The Law of the Garbage Truck makes this possible.

You are more kind, patient, and understanding when you graciously let other people's inconsequential mistakes pass you by. Refrain from judging others, as you would want them to refrain from judging you. You are on the right path when your loss helps you offer compassion to others who might be suffering as much as you are.

Authenticity

SOME PEOPLE CLAIM THAT IT IS SIMPLY NOT A REALISTIC OR AN AUTHENTIC expression of human emotion to expect people to honor their No Garbage Trucks! Pledge during their darkest hours. If you're mad, you should be mad. If you're sad, you should be sad. If you're depressed, you should be depressed. This is where the question of authenticity needs to be broadened.

The notion that we should bow to our first emotions is shortsighted. Authenticity does not require that we pull the behavioral trigger on every emotion we feel. What is more authentic, your inclination to show your anger to everyone following a great loss, or your desire to show compassion to those who may be suffering or challenged in their own lives? Human beings are not one emotion. We are a combination of emotions. Sometimes the second and third emotions we feel following an incident better represent the good people we are than the first emotion we feel.

"Living on automatic also places us at risk of mindlessly reacting to situations without reflecting on various options of response," says Daniel Siegel, codirector of the UCLA Mindful Awareness Research Institute, and author of *The Mindful Brain.* "The result can often be knee-jerk reactions that in turn initiate similar mindless reflexes in others. A cascade of reinforcing mindlessness can create a world of thoughtless interactions, cruelty, and destruction."

Remaining committed to living in a No Garbage Trucks! Zone helps you choose how to react to your feelings and how you can treat others positively.

The key is to be clear on what is important to you. When you are clear about your roles in life, and when you are grateful to serve in those roles, you know what to expect of yourself.

For the rest of your life, you may have moments when you are overwhelmed with sadness about having lost someone you love, or with concern for someone who is ill. Respect these emotions, and know that they are natural and to be expected. These emotions should not be denied—they are a part of you, but they do not define you.

While your pain may feel as if it is too much to bear at times, psychologist George Bonanno's research is a reminder that the intensity of your distress will ease over time. Your pain will be interrupted by feelings of happiness in other areas of your life, and the burden of your loss will weigh less heavily on you.

However, if your pain is constant, you must reach out for help. Get the support you need. See a counselor. Seek spiritual guidance. Do whatever is needed to help you do more than survive. Even in your darkest hours, help is available. You only have to ask for it, and be willing to accept it. You need to do whatever works for you. You deserve a beautiful life, and it's within your grasp.

Your Action Guide

Pay attention to the way you react to people and events that bother you. Do you take a narrow view of the situation, act like a Garbage Truck, and justify your negative behavior? Or do you take a broad view of the circumstance and try to consider everyone involved before you respond?

This week, make a commitment to avoid acting on the first negative emotion you feel the next time something upsets you. Promise yourself to take a broad view of the situation—think of everyone involved—before you act. Then write below how good it feels to act, instead, on your more thoughtful—and just as authentic—positive emotions.

CHAPTER TWENTY-NINE

Think You Can't Change?

A man, though wise, should never be ashamed
of learning more, and must unbend his mind.

—Sophocles

IN MY WORK AS A WRITER, SPEAKER, AND SEMINAR LEADER, I HAVE MET people from all over the world who claim they cannot change. They say that living in a No Garbage Trucks! Zone is too hard, that it's beyond their capacity. If you or someone you know feels this way, I have good news: Science demonstrates that the opposite is true. You *can* change. You *can* be happier.

Psychologist and researcher Sonja Lyubomirsky's "Sustainable Happiness Model," which she developed with psychologists Ken Sheldon and David Schkade, illustrates that you are not a slave to your genetic makeup. You *can* influence your happiness.

Lyubomirsky and her colleagues found that only "50 percent of the differences among people's happiness levels can be accounted for by their genetically determined *set points*." The researchers also found that just "ten percent of the variance in our happiness levels is explained by differences in life circumstances or situations—that is, whether we are rich or poor, healthy or unhealthy, beautiful or plain, married or divorced, etc."

So this means that if we all had the same genes and circumstances in our lives, we would still find that a full 40 percent of our differences in our happiness levels are due to the choices we make. And if you believe, as I do, that we can often improve our circumstances, we can up our percentage of control to nearly 50 percent. That's exciting news.

I wrote *The Law of the Garbage Truck* to help you make the most of your 50 percent.

Your Action Guide

When you want something to be better in your life, you have to work at it. Change requires effort, and change is possible. Science confirms it.

Write below how knowing that change is possible—that you can learn to live in a No Garbage Trucks! Zone—helps you improve, and how it will help you support others.

THE EIGHTH COMMITMENT

Do Declare Your Work a No Garbage Trucks! Zone

THE NEXT QUESTION TO CONSIDER IS HOW TO EXPAND YOUR NO GARBAGE Trucks! Zone from your personal to your professional life. The opportunity would be significant if you could, because you have the potential to influence hundreds, maybe thousands, of people through your job and career. In fact, people are already doing it all over the world. You don't have to be the president or CEO to have an impact on your company. You can make a difference.

CHAPTER THIRTY

Working in a No Garbage Trucks! Zone

*Every action done in company ought to be done
with some sign of respect to those that are present.*

—George Washington

THINK OF THE NUMBER OF PEOPLE YOU INTERACT WITH EVERY DAY. HOW many people do you work with? How many people pass by your cubicle or office? How many people come into your store? How many people do you visit? How many meetings do you attend? How many customers do you support? How many e-mails do you send and receive? How many calls do you make and answer? When you consider all the people you touch every day, your decision to work in a No Garbage Trucks! Zone will have a direct and positive impact on many.

Emotional Contagion

IF YOU BELIEVE, AS I DO, IN A BEHAVIORAL RIPPLE EFFECT IN LIFE—THAT AN interaction with Person A will influence his or her interaction with Person B, who will influence Person C, and so on—you will understand that we have a great responsibility to others in how we choose to act in the world. Scientists refer to this ripple effect as "emotional contagion."

In their book *Emotional Contagion*, psychologists Elaine Hatfield, John Cacioppo, and Richard Rapson present compelling evidence, "(1) that people tend to mimic others; (2) that emotional experience is affected by such feedback; and (3) that people therefore tend to 'catch' others' emotions." The researchers make it clear that people influence us with their emotions, and we influence them with ours. These findings serve as a reminder not to spread our unnecessary negative emotions to others, and to reinforce the importance of choosing to work in a No Garbage Trucks! Zone.

Three Degrees of Influence

SOCIAL CONTAGION RESEARCHER, SOCIOLOGIST, AND MEDICAL DOCTOR Nicholas Christakis and his colleague, political scientist James Fowler, discovered that our behavior influences people within three degrees of us. They call this phenomenon the Three Degrees of Influence Rule, in which "Everything we do or say tends to ripple through our network." When you consider the number of interactions you have on a daily basis, you have the power to alter the experience of thousands of people each day. In their book *Connected*, Christakis and Fowler write:

> Even when restricted to three degrees, the extent of our effect on others is extraordinary. . . . For example, suppose you have twenty social contacts, including five friends, five coworkers, and ten family members, and each of them in turn has similar numbers of friends and family. . . . That means you are indirectly connected to four hundred people at two degrees of separation. And your influence doesn't stop there; it goes one more step to the twenty friends and family of each of those people, yielding a total of 20 x 20 x 20 people, or eight thousand people who are three degrees removed from you.

Knowing how connected we truly are, we must help others become carriers of our positive energy, not Garbage Trucks burdened with our negative energy. Given how the scourge of incivility is taking a toll on workplace productivity, we must commit to working in a No Garbage Trucks! Zone.

Incivility at Work

ACCORDING TO CHRISTINE PEARSON AND CHRISTINE PORATH, MANAGEMENT researchers and professors who coauthored *The Cost of Bad Behavior,*

96 percent of workers have experienced incivility at work; 80 percent believe incivility is a problem; 60 percent experience stress because of workplace incivility; 48 percent are treated uncivilly at work at least once a week; and 75 percent of employees are dissatisfied with the way their companies handle incivility. The problem is even worse because 94 percent of employees get even with their offenders, and 88 percent get even with their organizations.

People are distracted by rude behavior and are less productive as a result. Pearson and Porath point to the economic burden of incivility: "Incivility's measurable costs alone are enormous. Job stress, for instance, costs U.S. corporations $300 billion a year, much of which has been shown to stem from workplace incivility." Furthermore, 94 percent of all those who experience incivility describe their negative encounter to someone else. In their paper "Assessing and Attacking Workplace Incivility," Pearson, Porath, and fellow researcher Lynne Andersson conclude, "When uncivil incidents are overlooked, the target suffers, the instigator thrives, and the organization loses." Simply stated, incivility is a powerful contributor to The Garbage Cycle at work.

Negative Energizers

KIM CAMERON, A UNIVERSITY OF MICHIGAN PSYCHOLOGIST AND cofounder of the Center for Positive Organizational Scholarship, reviews research about the detrimental impact "negative energizers" have in an organization in his book *Positive Leadership.* He writes, "Negative energizers deplete the good feelings and enthusiasm of others. They sap strength and weaken people. They leave others feeling exhausted and diminished. Negative energizers have been found to be critical, inflexible, selfish, and untrustworthy."

Establishing Your Zones

THE QUESTION THEN IS, HOW CAN YOU REMAIN FREE OF THE UNDUE influence of Garbage Trucks? How can you communicate to others that you work in a No Garbage Trucks! Zone? If you do not have people reporting to you, how can you spread the message at work? Here is an example of what one person is doing.

Tamara Cooper processes disability applications and manages disability cases for an organization in Maine. In 2006 she began creating her own No Garbage Trucks! Zone at work:

I was having a difficult time with a customer. It wasn't so much what the customer was asking of me; it was how she was asking it—with contempt and in a demeaning way. I always helped her, but her approach left me feeling bad each time. After you told me about The Law of the Garbage Truck, I decided I would smile inside whenever this customer would call. I would think, "Okay, I see a Garbage Truck coming my way." It was sort of my inside joke. It made it easier for me to hear the customer's requests without paying attention to the way they were made. That shift in my thinking made all the difference.

That's when I began sharing The Law with several of my coworkers. I actually e-mailed The Law to them and received several responses. Everyone was very excited and interested in it. I even shared The Law on DVD with my boss. She watched it and was impressed with the message.

The Law of the Garbage Truck came up several times a month in our conversations at work. We would share the difficulties we were having and remind each other that these were perfect situations for practicing The Law. When I received angry phone calls at work, I would get off the phone and say, "Another chance to practice The Law." It became a fun part of our day. The work we do in our department is often with people who are scared, sick, angry, and dealing with the unexpected danger of losing pieces of their lives. Some of them turn their anger on us, so we have many opportunities to practice The Law of the Garbage Truck. We have an understanding in the office that we will support and not dump garbage on each other.

Tamara's story demonstrates that when you agree to work in a No Garbage Trucks! Zone, you can trust each other to communicate thoughtfully, respectfully, and fairly.

Expressing frustration is natural, and it can even be productive if you don't turn your frustration into bad behavior and dump on your coworkers, customers, and bosses. The key is to share your concerns without becoming a Garbage Truck.

Spreading the Message

WHEN I WAS DIRECTOR OF LEARNING AND DEVELOPMENT AT YAHOO!, I would keep copies of books I liked and wanted people to know about on my desk. If I *really* liked a book, I'd loan them out or just give them away to anyone who asked about them. The books were always related to a message I wanted to communicate or an initiative I was leading. Sometimes I found it easier to get my message across by sharing someone else's writing. I've continued this practice in my own business. Some of the books I'm handing out these days are listed in the Notes and References section.

It doesn't take much to begin extending your No Garbage Trucks! Zone at work. Since everyone can relate to The Law of the Garbage Truck, it's easy to share with the people you know. Just leave a copy of this book on your desk and see what happens.

Your Action Guide

Visualize all the important people in your organization. How will living in a No Garbage Trucks! Zone help you improve your relationships with these key people? What will be different in the way you interact with them?

Write below the example you will set for others.

CHAPTER THIRTY-ONE

Leading in a No Garbage Trucks! Zone

The secret of success is constancy to purpose.

—Benjamin Disraeli

EVERYONE CAN WORK IN A NO GARBAGE TRUCKS! ZONE. YOU CAN MAKE the choice and do it. You don't need permission. You can make a difference in your company, no matter what your job is.

If you're a leader in your organization now or plan to be in the future, you can do even more. You can set expectations that you will have sound strategic planning, effective goal setting, strengths-based job alignment, proper training, timely communication, thoughtful reward programs, and regular check-ins with employees. You can also determine that certain things are non-negotiable. You can declare that acting like a Garbage Truck on a regular basis is not acceptable, because we all know Garbage Trucks are bad for business. They place an undue strain on our relationships, and they distract us from carrying out our mission.

Spirited Debate

IT IS CRITICAL TO REMIND EVERYONE IN YOUR ORGANIZATION THAT YOU CAN talk about anything in a No Garbage Trucks! Zone. You can debate, be fierce in your opinions, and even attack another person's ideas, as long as you don't attack the person. Focus on the issues: Agree to have what I call a "spirited debate," not an argument.

A spirited debate is issue-centered. You put everyone's ideas on the table and intelligently and passionately discuss them until you arrive at a solution. Arguing, on the other hand, frequently descends into personal attacks. Once you allow an argument to become personal, you invoke people's most basic defenses, and they focus on protecting themselves, not discussing the issues. This is how arguments degenerate into how best to weaken your opponents personally, not how to undercut their arguments. In his autobiography, *Long Walk to Freedom*, Nelson Mandela recounts a lesson he learned early in life: "I learned that to humiliate another person is to make him suffer an unnecessarily cruel fate. Even as a boy, I defeated my opponents without dishonoring them."

Communication Preference

THE ETIQUETTE OF DEBATE IS SIMPLE IF YOU DECIDE BEFOREHAND HOW the discussion will be conducted. Allowing time to consider the way people communicate will help keep the conversation focused on content, not personalities. Remember that people express themselves differently. Some raise their voices when they're excited, and some feel that good ideas can't be generated unless there's conflict; some prefer being direct, even if it makes them appear insensitive; while others prefer to remain calm, deliver their criticism gently, and generally hold the belief that good ideas are all too easily drowned out with too much conflict.

Living in a democracy—whether in our nations or workplaces—requires that we give one another the opportunity to express ourselves openly and passionately. We just need to be respectful when we do it.

In another story from *Long Walk to Freedom*, Mandela reminds us that we can have a disagreement without being disagreeable. In his description of President George H. W. Bush, he writes: "He was a man with whom one could disagree and then shake hands."

In that same spirit, Yale University Law professor Stephen Carter reflects on how the civil rights movement in the United States "wanted to expand American democracy, not destroy it, and [Martin Luther] King understood that uncivil dialogue serves no democratic function."

In another passage from his book *Civility: Manners, Morals, and the Etiquette of Democracy*, Carter urges us to keep the lines of communication open with everyone, including the people with whom we disagree:

Indeed, the more passionate our certainty that we are right, the more urgent our need to practice the art of civility—otherwise, we make dialogue impossible, and the possibility of dialogue is the reason democracy values disagreement in the first place.

If civil rights marchers, threatened with fire hoses, police dogs, terrorist bombs, and assassins' bullets, could be civil in their dissent against a system willing and ready to destroy them, it is laughable to suggest that the rest of us, facing far lesser tribulations, lack that capacity. For those who believe in dialogue, then, hypocrisy lies in the pretense that we can discuss our differences seriously without the aid of civility.

The Bullying Epidemic

THE PREVALENCE OF ONE OF THE WORST FORMS OF WORKPLACE INCIVILITY—bullying—was made glaringly evident in a survey conducted in 2007 by the Workplace Bullying Institute (WBI) and the polling firm Zogby International. WBI founders Gary and Ruth Namie estimated that 54 million Americans have been bullied at work. The team's 2003 WBI survey found that the effects of this mistreatment are significant: 94 percent of bullied targets suffer from severe anxiety, 84 percent from sleep disruption, 82 percent from loss of concentration, and 80 percent from feeling edgy and easily startled, not to mention those who suffer from stress, headaches, body aches, and depression.

The Namies discovered something even more worrying about the bullying epidemic. When "bullied targets" (people like you and me) report the abuse to their companies, 18 percent of the time the problem is made worse, and 44 percent of the time nothing is done.

This is why it is absolutely critical to establish No Garbage Trucks! Zones in our organizations. We need to make it clear that incivility, and bullying in particular, is unacceptable. Establishing No Garbage Trucks! Zones is akin to implementing a zero likelihood policy—you reduce bad behavior by educating people not to live as Garbage Trucks. Living in the Zone also supports a zero tolerance policy, where people are held accountable for dumping their garbage.

The First Move

BUILDING TRUST AMONG TEAM MEMBERS IN AN ORGANIZATION IS ONE OF the most important responsibilities of a leader. Employees need to feel that they understand the rules of the game and that the rules are applied fairly. They need to believe that the organization is looking out for their interests and that they have the support of their team members.

While a leader is responsible for setting performance and behavioral expectations—how we treat our customers, suppliers, partners, and each other—positive working cultures are best determined with employee involvement. When employees have a stake in the rules, they are more likely to follow and enforce them. Asking employees to help establish a No Garbage Trucks! Zone is a powerful first step. Here's how it works.

Ask the team to help define what accepting and dumping garbage in the organization looks and feels like. What is considered dumping to the group? Talk about it. Find out what is out of bounds and what is acceptable. Talk about what it feels like when dumping occurs, and how good it feels to avoid it. Ask team members to grant one another permission to call each other out—kindly and respectfully—when they're dumping. And make sure everyone understands the difference between venting (which is permission-based and time-sensitive) and dumping.

It is also important to help team members identify when they should let Garbage Trucks pass by. There are always predictable interactions with customers, suppliers, partners, and employees of other departments that should be put in perspective. People say things that do not always warrant a response. Their comments are better left alone so that the energy of the interaction can remain focused on resolving the issue, not wasting time on perceived slights. Naming the most obvious and common examples of unimportant provocations helps everyone. Team members will be better centered as they enter and navigate these typical interactions; they will feel better and be more effective; they will return to the team with more positive energy; and they will leave customers, partners, and employees from other departments more satisfied.

A Worthy Investment

SOME LEADERS ARE FEARFUL OF OPENING UP THIS TYPE OF CONVERSATION. They're afraid of how it might be received. Will their employees participate openly? Will they support each other? Will they commit to working through issues as they arise? Ultimately, a leader wants to know that talking openly about communication will be worth the effort.

My experience consulting leaders—and my own history with leadership—confirms that teams positively respond to a leader's overture if the leader is sincere and if the leader is committed to following up (drive-by initiatives are rarely appreciated). The investment of time it takes for a team to establish and personalize a No Garbage Trucks! Zone is far less than the time it takes to continually firefight the negative interactions among team members who do not share the same understanding and commitment to civil communication. "Shared values regularize behavior within a group in an efficient way," writes psychologist Christopher Peterson in his book *A Primer in Positive Psychology*, "by articulating a general rule that applies broadly, so group members are spared the ongoing reinvention of standards and their justifications."

The Eight Steps

AS A LEADER IN A NO GARBAGE TRUCKS! ZONE, THERE ARE EIGHT STEPS you must follow in order to make sure your team members are honoring their No Garbage Trucks! Commitments. The first six steps should always be followed. Pursue the last two only if needed.

1. Set expectations and make sure that they are *clear* to everyone.

2. Ask each team member if the expectations are *understood*; if there's any confusion, discuss them further.

3. Keep your own behavior *consistent* with the expectations.

4. *Recognize* and *celebrate* behavior consistent with the expectations.

5. Give honest and direct *feedback* when the expectations are not met.

6. Provide *development*—coaching and training—if a member of your team is struggling to meet the expectations.

7. *Reassign* team members to positions that allow them to meet the expectations.

8. Allow employees to *resign*, or *dismiss* them, if they cannot meet the expectations.

If you follow the first six steps and you are still not successful, your employees will not be surprised if you pursue number seven; they will understand that reassigning them is your only remaining option before terminating their employment. If the eighth step is made necessary, the employees in question will realize that they have chosen an unacceptable path, and you must let them go. Your mission is to preserve your organization's ability to thrive in the Zone—where no one regularly dumps or accepts garbage.

The Four Keys to Good Feedback

HOW YOU GIVE INPUT TO YOUR EMPLOYEES AND TEAM MEMBERS IS CRITICAL to the success of your relationships. If you do it right, your relationships will flourish. (You are appreciated when you give compassionate, supportive, and honest feedback.) Do it wrong and your relationships will suffer. (You are viewed as a Garbage Truck, ready to dump ungrounded, unbalanced, and unfair judgment on people.)

Also remember that people want your praise to be thoughtful and grounded. No one values empty flattery. When you give evidence for your compliments, you demonstrate sincerity and you communicate what you value.

Here are the Four Keys to Good Feedback in a No Garbage Trucks! Zone:

1. *Ask permission* to share feedback. You'll always get it, and the fact that you respectfully asked for permission will center the person's attention on what you have to share.

2. Briefly *state your expectations* of the person's performance or behavior.

3. Objectively *describe what happened.* If someone else can confirm what you saw or heard, your message will be even stronger.

4. *Describe the impact* of the behavior or event. What were the results? Tell the person why it matters.

Make sure that your feedback is timely, factual, balanced, and delivered with good intentions. You need your team members to achieve what is expected of them. You want your input to be embraced, not dismissed as garbage. Giving constructive and productive feedback is your team's expectation of you.

The blessing and the burden of leadership is that you must set expectations and continually hold people accountable to them. With so many issues constantly demanding your attention, you need efficient and effective ways of communicating and reminding everyone how you will treat each other and work together. Your values must always be clear.

Your Action Guide

This week, do three things.

Answer this question: How would your team benefit if you pulled them together to personalize a No Garbage Trucks! Zone for your organization? Write below your answer in two or three sentences.

Take time this week to acknowledge someone at work whom you have not adequately recognized. Be specific. Follow the Four Keys to Good Feedback. Write below how good you feel after you've communicated your well-grounded praise.

Additionally, take time to address someone at work who is not meeting expectations. Be specific. Follow the Four Keys to Good Feedback. Write below how you feel after you deliver your evidence-based feedback.

You are working in a No Garbage Trucks! Zone when you give timely, fair, and factual feedback to the people in your organization.

CHAPTER THIRTY-TWO

Declaring a No Garbage Trucks! Zone in Your Organization

That is the principal thing: not to remain within the dream, with the intention, with the being in the mood, but always forcibly to convert it into all things.

—Rainer Maria Rilke

I WROTE *THE LAW OF THE GARBAGE TRUCK* TO HELP SHIFT OUR consciousness about happiness, success, and civility. It's not enough for us to learn how to listen better, give feedback, resolve conflicts more effectively, and handle difficult people. Although these are valuable skills, it is more important that we reach a deeper level of awareness to affect real change in our organizations. We must appeal to each other's humanity to understand that acting like a Garbage Truck hurts our organizations and makes work less enjoyable. Positive psychology research suggests how important it is to work in a No Garbage Trucks! Zone.

The Research

IN A SERIES OF STUDIES, PSYCHOLOGISTS BARBARA FREDRICKSON and Marcial Losada found that when business team members communicate with one another in a ratio of three or more positive and constructive comments to every negative and unproductive comment, they are predictably more successful, as measured by profitability, customer satisfaction, and evaluations by superiors, peers, and subordinates. This is not to say that successful teams in the study avoided confrontation and debate, rather they focused more on "inquiry" (trying to understand each other's ideas and positions) than on "advocacy" (trying to convince everyone that they were right). The successful work teams were also more likely to show "support, encouragement, or appreciation" of their team members, rather than "disapproval, sarcasm, or cynicism."

Declaring that your organizations are No Garbage Trucks! Zones is part of a critical business strategy to keep positivity high and negativity low. It's a key factor in helping organizations stay focused on what matters.

Examples

OVER THE YEARS I'VE HAD THE PRIVILEGE OF SHARING THE LAW OF THE Garbage Truck philosophy with many great companies and organizations. The leaders of these organizations have taken different approaches to implementing The Law of the Garbage Truck, and each effort has been equally impressive. I'm proud of their accomplishments. To give you an idea of how your organization might benefit from working in a No Garbage Trucks! Zone, I offer you a few of their stories.

The United States Veterans Health Administration: The Civility, Respect, and Engagement in the Workplace Program

THE VETERANS HEALTH ADMINISTRATION (VHA) IS RESPONSIBLE FOR THE healthcare mission of the United States Department of Veterans Affairs (VA), and operates VA outpatient clinics, hospitals, medical centers, and long-term healthcare facilities.

The footprint of the VHA is enormous. Consider these statistics: In 2008 alone, 5.5 million people received care in a VA healthcare facility. More than 50 percent of doctors practicing in the United States received at least a portion of their professional education in the VA healthcare system. A quarter of a million employees work for the VHA.

If you think again about the ripple effect of one person's impact on another—remember Christakis and Fowler's Three Degrees of Influence Rule—the VHA's reach into the world is even larger than the numbers indicate. When VHA employees are at their best, they positively influence the patients they serve, as well as the patients' families, friends, and colleagues who visit, love, and care for them. This is why the VHA launched the Civility, Respect, and Engagement in the Workplace (CREW) program in 2004.

The CREW program was initiated to raise the level of communication, teamwork, trust, and respect among employees in the organization. The intended outcomes were improved patient satisfaction, increased staff engagement, reduced sick leave, and reduced equal employment opportunity complaints. "Civility, respect, and engagement are foundational to our mission at the Veteran's Health Administration, not fluff," says Linda Belton, C.H.E., VHA Director of Organizational Health, and one of the founders of the CREW program. "Everything we do is connected to everything and to everyone. What we do every day matters."

VHA staff members, who are trained to facilitate work groups of their colleagues—doctors, nurses, administrators, food service personnel, and maintenance employees—lead the CREW program. Facilitators help guide their groups to achieve the CREW mission of creating a better workplace for everyone.

In 2008, at the request of CREW facilitators, the VHA decided to make "The Law of the Garbage Truck" available to CREW participants nationwide. The facilitators recognized The Law as an important tool for improving employee satisfaction, productivity, and patient services.

JoAnne Renz, R.N., M.S.N, is the CREW coordinator for the Coatesville, Pennsylvania, VA Medical Center. In 2007, she brought The Law to the attention of the national CREW program.

> I remember the first time I used The Law of the Garbage Truck with a CREW group. As in probably most all work groups, there were some staff members who could be called "actively disengaged." These staff members felt they or one of their coworkers had been "done wrong" in the past. Rather than try to contribute to building the environment desired by the group, the disgruntled staff members kept sharing their personal horror stories and generalized negativity. That's when I used facilitator's privilege to stand up in front of them, and with feeling, read them "The Law of the Garbage Truck." And it was beautiful. The group acknowledged that although there will always be garbage, they don't have to let other people's garbage keep them from what's important in their lives.

The results of the CREW program have been outstanding. Employees have become more emotionally engaged at work, customer service has increased, equal employment opportunity complaints have dropped, the number of sick days has declined, and employee retention has risen. Increased civility in the workplace has led to the achievement of significant business outcomes. "CREW is more than a training program; it's a way of doing business," says Belton.

Although the CREW program was successful before the introduction of The Law of the Garbage Truck, the VHA has clearly strengthened its ability to increase civility, respect, and engagement in the workplace by making The Law available to all facilitators and their CREW groups.

Warner Bros. Entertainment: Home of Batman and Harry Potter

WARNER BROS. IS ONE OF THE MOST SUCCESSFUL AND CELEBRATED entertainment companies in the world. *Batman* and the Harry Potter movie series alone have generated billions of dollars at the box office.

Additional millions are earned each year from the licensing of the rights to the names, likenesses, and logos of all the intellectual properties in the Warner Bros. vast film and television library. With more than 3,700 active licensees worldwide, Warner Bros. Consumer Products calls upon leaders like Preston Kevin Lewis to run their licensing business. A veteran of Disney, MTV, and HBO Home Video, Lewis is the Managing Director of Warner Bros. Consumer Products for Australia and New Zealand. Assuming his post in 2007, Lewis is responsible for the day-to-day operations, sales, marketing, retail, promotions, and licensing activity in the region.

Although Warner Bros. had a successful business in the region, there was a significant opportunity to grow the business when Lewis took over. He understood that new business strategies were necessary and that new customer programs would be critical to implement. He also believed that any improvements made to the business would be sustained only if the culture supported them. Therefore, Lewis had his staff read "The Law of the Garbage Truck." He wanted everyone to share the same language and put into practice the No Garbage Trucks! philosophy. Lewis said, "The best thing that I have found about the Law of the Garbage Truck is that it keeps people from being distracted with negative thoughts, issues, and behaviors, and focuses them on driving results."

Lewis made a decision that everything to do with business could be discussed and debated, but acting like Garbage Trucks in the workplace would not be allowed. He knew that bad moods, attitudes, and behaviors would keep them from achieving their important business outcomes. He also knew that work would not be fun if everyone was weighed down by Garbage Trucks.

"A part of this process also means that everyone can't be saved—some are not able to rise to the level that The Law of the Garbage Truck demands," said Lewis. "If people insist on acting like Garbage Trucks, they have to find another organization. The people in our organization love what they do and are committed to helping others be their best. We need everyone pulling together to meet our results."

New Age Transportation: Success and an Award-winning CEO

CAROLYN GABLE IS THE CEO OF NEW AGE TRANSPORTATION, DISTRIBUTION & Warehousing Inc., a Lake Zurich, Illinois-based, $30 million company she founded out of her townhouse in 1989. A single mother of seven, ages 9 to 34, Gable's rags to riches story has frequently attracted the media's attention. She is a recipient of the Ernst & Young Entrepreneur of the Year Award and the author of *Everything I Know as a CEO, I Learned as a Waitress*. In 2008, Gable integrated The Law of the Garbage Truck and The No Garbage Trucks! Pledge into her family and business.

It started when Gable's daughter-in-law came to a family dinner and wanted to talk about something she had just read: It was "The Law of the Garbage Truck."

Months after that dinner, Gable participated in a session I led about the power of The Law of the Garbage Truck. She testified in my session to the power of The Law by describing the positive impact it had had on her own family. She then declared that she intended to take it to her other family, the employees of New Age Transportation.

At her company's annual kickoff meeting, everyone watched The Law of the Garbage Truck and The No Garbage Trucks! Pledge DVDs.

Afterward, Gable asked all of her employees to do what thousands of employees in other companies had done before them. She had them stand together and take The No Garbage Trucks! Pledge. They threw themselves into it, had fun, and committed to running their business—serving their customers and helping each other—without acting like Garbage Trucks. Gable describes it this way:

> The No Garbage Trucks! Pledge is a mantra my family and employees have continued to recite many months after we first learned it and committed to it. Taking The Pledge in my company reminded all of us that we don't have to take on other people's negative stuff!
>
> We have to enjoy our moments and not let others dump their emotional garbage on us! We also have to commit to not dumping on others. It's our choice to make. We can all live and work in a No Garbage Trucks! Zone.

Steel Magnolias Breast Cancer Support Group, Inc.: Changing Legislation to Save Lives

LENORA JOHNSON IS THE FOUNDER AND EXECUTIVE DIRECTOR OF THE Alabama-based Steel Magnolias Breast Cancer Support Group. She is also a breast cancer survivor.

A friend of Johnson's, the director of a residential treatment center for those addicted to alcohol and drugs, asked Johnson to read "The Law of the Garbage Truck." Johnson listened to her friend. She read The Law, and then wrote to me.

> I recently read your "Law of the Garbage Truck." I couldn't get it off my mind. I wanted to share it with everyone in the Steel Magnolias network. It reminded me that we never achieve anything when we let the negative things get in our way. There will always be a barrage of people who will derail us if we're not focused.

Johnson knows what she's talking about. Her work with the Alabama State Legislature proves it. Johnson and the Steel Magnolias team led a grassroots effort to close a loophole in Alabama state law. Steel Magnolias had discovered that if a woman received a breast cancer diagnosis from her own doctor she would not qualify for treatment from the state. The law required that a woman first go to the Alabama Health Department to receive her diagnosis, but that was not always possible. Steel Magnolias knew that this law had to change. Women were being locked out of the treatment they needed. As a result of their perseverance and the support of key lawmakers, the law was changed. On April 30, 2009, after having passed the Alabama House of Representatives and Senate unanimously, Alabama Governor Bob Riley signed HB147 into law.

"We would never have pushed through that legislation if we had let Garbage Trucks get in our way. When we were between a rock and a hard place, we kept our faith. We pursued our goal with tunnel vision."

Johnson remains on a mission. She has seen the power of purpose and focus. "I want to do so much more. We can make an even greater difference in the lives of so many women. We just can't afford to let Garbage Trucks run us over. We also can't be Garbage Trucks. Our mission is too important."

Your Action Guide

Think about your organization. What steps could you take to create a No Garbage Trucks! Zone? Whose help would you need? What resources would you need? What obstacles would you have to overcome?

Write below two things you could do this week to help you start implementing a No Garbage Trucks! Zone in your organization.

CHAPTER THIRTY-THREE

The Courage of Your Commitment

What lies behind us and what lies before us are
tiny matters compared to what lies within us.

—Ralph Waldo Emerson

I KNOW MANY ORGANIZATIONS THAT HAVE COMMITTED TO WORKING AND living in a No Garbage Trucks! Zone, and they're all successful. Now it's your turn.

This is the right moment to declare every area of your life—home, school, work, and community—a No Garbage Trucks! Zone. You now have the power, motivation, and resolve to focus on what you truly care about.

Declaring that your life is a No Garbage Trucks! Zone takes courage. The crowd will not always move in your direction; some people will continue to focus on their frustration, anger, and disappointment. Others will prefer to gossip, criticize, and complain. This is the reason you have to be a leader and set an example. You have to remain steady in your commitment to live a life free of the influence of Garbage Trucks.

Your Action Guide

You deserve to work in a No Garbage Trucks! Zone. Your coworkers deserve to work in a No Garbage Trucks! Zone. But it takes your declaration and your commitment to implement one.

Write below what will give you the courage to follow through and establish a No Garbage Trucks! Zone.

CHAPTER THIRTY-FOUR

Great Change Is Possible

Here am I; send me.

—Isaiah 6:8

STANFORD UNIVERSITY PROFESSOR EMERITUS PHILIP ZIMBARDO, BEST KNOWN for a classic psychology study conducted at Stanford in 1971 (The Stanford Prison Experiment) and author of *The Lucifer Effect: Understanding How Good People Turn Evil,* cautions us to be wary of the creeping influence of evil:

> *Be discouraged from venal sins and small transgressions, such as cheating, lying, gossiping, spreading rumors, laughing at racist or sexist jokes, teasing, and bullying. They can become stepping-stones to more serious falls from grace. They serve as mini-facilitators for thinking and acting destructively against your fellow creatures.*

Zimbardo's cautionary words are in keeping with living in a No Garbage Trucks! Zone, where the expectation is that you will not succumb to the negative forces around you, or submit to those whose intent is to draw you into uncaring, inconsiderate, and hurtful behavior. It takes strength not to give in to people who are committed to inflicting pain—physical or emotional—on you or anyone else, and it takes courage to reject the power of tyrants and bullies.

At the same time, your No Garbage Trucks! Pledge compels you to be gracious and forgiving of the insignificant mistakes of others—the same mistakes for which you would want to be pardoned. You can choose to de-escalate a situation by removing your attention from it, and instead, focus on what matters. You don't have to accept garbage.

Your pledge also compels you not to dump garbage on others. Everyone deserves the freedom to live a good life. But your freedom does not include the right to become a tyrant or bully. Instead, embrace the challenge of winning people over to your side with the power of your moral purpose. Be clear on what you value, and be prepared to support it.

Rising Above

GREAT LEADERS KNOW THAT THEY CANNOT LET OTHERS DETERMINE THEIR moods and behaviors. They take responsibility for how they feel and what they do. Without this commitment, their mission to bring about a more just, free, and compassionate world would not be possible.

Nelson Mandela survived twenty-seven years in prison in part because he did not allow his jailors—everyone from the country's political leaders to the guards at the prison—to dump their garbage on him and break his spirit. Mandela could not control the behavior of his oppressors, but he could determine the way their unjust and cruel treatment would affect him.

Mandela had every right to become bitter and feel hatred for all those who deprived him of his liberty. But he kept his faith that one day he would help bring freedom and equality to all South Africans. He did not avoid conflict upon his release from prison. He successfully navigated it. Mandela reminds us all that we must not give in to hatred. He writes in his autobiography:

> I always knew that deep down in every human heart, there is mercy and generosity. No one is born hating another person because of the color of his skin, or his background, or his religion. People must learn to hate, and if they can learn to hate, they can be taught to love, for love comes more naturally to the human heart than its opposite. Even in the grimmest times in prison, when my comrades and I were pushed to our limits, I would see a glimmer of humanity in one of the guards, perhaps just for a second, but it was enough to reassure me and keep me going. Man's goodness is a flame that can be hidden but never extinguished.

Nelson Mandela followed the biblical commandment "Love your enemies, do good to those who hate you, bless those who curse you, and pray for those who spitefully use you." His conviction to do right guided his actions. Mandela exemplifies the spirit of The No Garbage Trucks! Pledge and the commitment to living in a No Garbage Trucks! Zone.

You too have a mission in life, and one life in which to achieve it.

There is no time to waste.

Your Action Guide

What problems in the world most concern you and seem beyond your influence?

What would happen if you let pass by the Garbage Trucks that say that change cannot happen? What if you stopped giving power to your bad memories and self-doubts? What if you stopped inventing catastrophes in your future? What if you followed Nelson Mandela's example, and set your mind to accomplishing what is important and what you know is right?

Write below what you could achieve in life if you turned your attention from Garbage Trucks to what is truly possible. Write down how you would make the world a better place for everyone.

CHAPTER THIRTY-FIVE

Together on a Mission

*Never doubt that a small group of thoughtful committed citizens
can change the world. Indeed, it is the only thing that ever has.*

—Margaret Mead

I HAVE TRAVELED, STUDIED, AND WORKED IN MORE THAN THIRTY-FIVE
countries. I have led seminars and spoken at international congresses
with delegates from over one hundred nations. My wife, Dawn, and I have
traveled with our daughters to ten countries. I have seen firsthand how
powerful it is when people of all nations and all faiths let Garbage Trucks
pass them by. People are kinder, more understanding, and more forgiving
in a No Garbage Trucks! Zone.

Declaring that you live and work in a No Garbage Trucks! Zone affirms
your commitment to be civil, forgo grudges, empathize with others, listen
well, and engage in productive discourse.

A More Beautiful World

WHEN YOU LIVE YOUR LIFE IN A NO GARBAGE TRUCKS! ZONE, YOU EXPERIENCE
the benefits every day. The things that used to bother you no longer do.
The negative things you cannot control don't burden you as they once did.
You feel free to focus on what matters in your life.

Each time you let a Garbage Truck pass you by, you take control of
your life. Each time you stop dumping garbage on other people, you
change the world.

Almost every day I receive notes from people who have taken control of their lives by following The Law. Organizations write to me about how they have committed to working in a No Garbage Trucks! Zone and how it has improved their business. I am inspired each time I read these stories.

It's Possible

YOU HAVE THE POWER TO CHANGE YOUR LIFE. YOU HAVE THE POWER TO change your organization.

Happiness is not out of reach. Civility is not dead. The Law of the Garbage Truck makes happiness and civility a possibility. One supports the other in a virtuous cycle. Increase civility, increase happiness. Increase happiness, increase civility.

You can do it. You have the power. It's not complex. It's not a secret. It's The Law of the Garbage Truck, the law that can make our lives better— and the world a more beautiful place.

You know what you need to do. You know your No Garbage Trucks! mission. Now, you must live it, and tell the people you care about.

Thank you for joining me on this journey.

Your Action Guide
Who will you tell?

Appendices

A Special No Garbage Trucks! Zone—Our Schools

Somebody had asked me, "What is the most important commandment in the Bible?" and I said, "Thou shalt not stand idly by?"

—Elie Wiesel

THERE IS ONE NO GARBAGE TRUCKS! ZONE I WISH WE COULD ESTABLISH immediately: our schools.

Schools achieve their mission when they educate our children and when they help develop good character. They fail when our children are distracted from learning and are allowed to hurt others. More than 58 million students, grades K–12, go to school every day in the United States, and more than a billion more around the world. They're members of our families. They live in our neighborhoods. We pass them on the street. Each one of us is affected by the experiences we have with them.

If a child has a good experience in school, families, friends, and communities benefit. If the experience is bad, everyone suffers.

Everywhere

IN THEIR BOOK *SAFE SCHOOL AMBASSADORS*, YOUTH EDUCATORS RICK Phillips, John Linney, and Chris Pack bring to light alarming statistics about the prevalence and extent of bullying in our schools. Here are three of the studies the authors cite:

- A 2007 study conducted by Stanford University and the Lucille Packard Children's Hospital found that 90 percent of elementary students have been bullied by their peers, and nearly 60 percent have participated in some type of bullying in the past year.

- A 2004 report on a five-year study of a diverse group of nearly nineteen hundred students in grades 8 through 12 offers some insights into how many students reported being:

  * Left out of activities: 67 percent (43 percent sometimes and 24 percent often)

  * Called names: 74 percent (47 percent sometimes and 27 percent often)

  * Teased: 62 percent (45 percent sometimes and 17 percent often)

  * Hit or kicked: 46 percent (35 percent sometimes and 11 percent often)

  * Threatened: 42 percent (33 percent sometimes and 9 percent often)

- In a 2002 study by the Families and Work Institute, 66 percent of youth said they had "been teased or gossiped about in a mean way at least once in the last month," and 25 percent have had this experience five times or more. Over half (57 percent) said they had "teased or gossiped about someone at least once," and 12 percent had done so five times or more in the past month.

The results of all this bullying take a significant toll on the children involved. Phillips, Linney, and Pack point to research that demonstrates the extent to which children suffer psychologically and physically: "In two studies published in the *British Medical Journal*, researchers found that abdominal pain, headaches, bedwetting, sleep problems, anxiety, insecurity, and depression were much more common in targeted children and aggressors. Interestingly, the rates of these symptoms were highest in those who were bullied *and* in turn bullied others. More recently, UCLA conducted a study of two thousand sixth graders and their teachers. The study reinforced earlier findings that the targets of mistreatment suffer a wide range of health problems, including headaches, stomachaches, and sleeplessness."

Bullying is not limited to schools and playgrounds—it's infecting our social media at an increasing rate and at all hours of the day. The Internet is particularly ripe for bullies because it gives them the means to post hurtful pictures, videos, and comments about their targets while the bullies' identities remain hidden or disguised. The old bully punched you in the stomach. The new bully hits you in the back.

Teaching The Law

RON WILBER KNOWS ABOUT BULLIES. HE'S A MIDDLE SCHOOL TEACHER at Western Pines Middle School in Palm Beach County, Florida. He knows the destructive influence of bullies in kids' lives, and he's doing something about it. He's teaching them The Law of the Garbage Truck.

For the last two years, Wilber starts each semester of his sixth, seventh, and eighth grade Spanish classes by reading The Law of the Garbage Truck to his students. He lets them know that Garbage Trucks are not allowed in his classroom. It is never okay to make fun of someone, start a rumor, or gossip. Wilber does not allow it, and he addresses anyone who insists on acting like a Garbage Truck.

Wilber knows he's in charge. He gets to set the rules. He wants his kids to be free of harmful distraction and to be centered on learning. This is the first part of the story.

Here's the second part. Ron Wilber comes to school each day with the expectation that his students will stick up for one another. He expects his kids to call out "Garbage Truck!" if they witness someone beginning to tease or bully someone. Having fun with each other is great. Causing harm to each other is off-limits. As soon as playfulness turns mean-spirited, someone has to call out "Garbage Truck!"

Wilber described the first time he shared The Law of the Garbage Truck with his class:

I talked about bullying. I told them how bullies are the ones who dump garbage on their victims. Bullies are Garbage Trucks. Then I asked, "Has anyone ever been picked on in front of others?" Of course a lot of hands went up. Then I asked, "And when you were picked on or laughed at, did you ever find that no one stuck up for you?" Again, they all had stories when they faced a bully alone. "How did it feel?" I asked. The answer was always the same: "terrible." It was then that I said, "From now on, if anyone is being bullied, you are required to help the person getting picked on. You are to holler out, 'Garbage Truck!' When you do, I will stop all classroom instruction until we deal with the issue."

Practicing The Law

WILBER BRINGS TO LIFE THE LESSON OF THE LAW OF THE GARBAGE TRUCK through role-playing in class. He asks someone to start a mock teasing of someone, and then he calls for the class to respond by calling out "Garbage Truck!" Wilber then turns to the target of the mock teasing and asks, "How did it feel to have somebody stick up for you?" The kids always respond the same way: "It feels great," they say.

Wilber's students get it. Not a day goes by without someone calling out "Garbage Truck." The students stop each other before their comments become hurtful. "All it takes is one person to call out 'Garbage Truck!' and the bully stops," says Wilber. "They realize their target is not alone. Their target has support. That's all it takes."

Wilber's experience in the classroom is affirmed by the findings of research psychologists Debra Pepler and Wendy Craig in their paper "Making a Difference in Bullying": "When peers intervene, they are successful in stopping bullying about half the time."

When children learn The Law of the Garbage Truck and take The No Garbage Trucks! Pledge, the probability that they will intervene on another student's behalf is increased. Teaching The Law to children is critical when you consider the sobering research that peers do not normally intervene when a classmate is bullied. In their paper "Observations of Bullying and Victimization in the School Yard," Pepler and Craig found that "Peers were

involved in some capacity during 85 percent of the bullying episodes. . . .
In 30 percent of the episodes, peers actively participated in the bullying
episode as an aggressor, and in 23 percent of the episodes peers just
witnessed the bullying interaction." The most disturbing statistic in the
study shows that peers intervened in just 13 percent of the incidents.

Wilber points out that calling out "Garbage Truck!" works because
it literally stops bullies in their tracks. Someone bears witness to a bullied
classmate and speaks out on his or her behalf. The bully then retreats after
being called out for taking his or her garbage and dumping it on someone
else. Wilber says it this way: "To have thirty students stop and stare at a
bully—when he has to defend himself, *and apologize*—is so intimidating
that the bully rarely repeats the offense."

Policies Brought to Life

ANTI-BULLYING POLICIES ARE A CRITICAL COMPONENT OF MAKING A SCHOOL
physically and psychologically safe for students. Everyone—not just
students and teachers, but administrators and parents—has to understand
what is acceptable behavior and what is not.

The challenge is that few students can easily recite a policy. That's
where The Law of the Garbage Truck comes in; it brings policies to life in an
easily understood and actionable way. Once students learn The Law of the
Garbage Truck, they take it everywhere they go—past school hallways and
classrooms and into their neighborhoods and homes.

Student Stories

WILBER RECENTLY ASKED HIS STUDENTS TO WRITE HOW THE LAW OF THE
Garbage Truck has made a difference in their lives. He asked them to share
their stories with me. Each one is inspiring. Here are three of them:

> *I've always considered myself an okay person. I go to church,*
> *and try to be a good student. But recently I've let myself slip. I've*
> *always noticed that something within me is missing. As the tension*
> *built (as it often does when the puzzle piece doesn't quite fit), I*
> *began lashing out at my friends, family, and random people. I get*

upset over the smallest things. Before *The Law of the Garbage Truck* reached me, I had driven away almost all the friends I had, and I talked badly about the ones that were left. Then, like a godsend, Mr. Wilber read your message, and it clicked. I was a Garbage Truck. I was gathering all the negativity I saw in the permanently half-empty glass and forcing it onto those who least deserved it. Your message changed me. Thank you for taking one more Garbage Truck off the road.

—Jacqueline, 13

One day after school I came home to find my mom and dad fighting. My dad was yelling at my mom because she didn't have a job yet, and that she wasn't supporting our family like he was. He didn't understand how much work it was to clean the floors, dust the furniture, wash the dishes and clothes, take care of the dog, and overall just be a mom. She had also been working in his office, paying bills, filing papers and such. He said it was nothing compared to what he was doing. While they were going at it, all of a sudden I yelled, "Garbage Truck!" They just looked at me and asked, "What does that mean?" I explained what it meant, and before they knew it they had stopped fighting. *The Law of the Garbage Truck* helped me make my parents stop fighting, and helped make them realize that their fight was about something stupid and pointless.

—Alec, 13

One day I was in my world cultures class and people were yelling at this kid. Then the teacher told everyone to stop, but it only got worse. I decided to stick up for him. I walked to the front of the class and said, "Garbage Trucks are only dumping their garbage because they are having a bad day." I made my point. People don't yell at that boy anymore. This has helped me because I've learned to be courageous and stick up for myself and other people.

—Stephanie, 11

Another Chance to Help

ADHERING TO THE LAW GIVES STUDENTS, TEACHERS, ADMINISTRATORS, and parents alike the opportunity to help a Garbage Truck when they witness one. After stepping in to stop a bullying incident and following the prescribed school policy, they can ask the bully, "What's causing you to be a Garbage Truck today? What's making you dump garbage on others?" It's an easy entry into a difficult conversation. Punishment alone is not the answer; we have to help children choose another way to live.

When we see kids letting Garbage Trucks get under their skin, we have another opportunity to help. We've all witnessed students lose their composure quickly and let others get to them. We can see how this only widens the target for bullies. They make themselves easy prey for continued and intensified abuse. That's when we can pull them aside and say, "You're not a Garbage Truck. Why are you accepting so much garbage today? What's making you so sensitive?"

Our questions open a window of opportunity to see if there is something we can do to help the child gain more confidence, be more at peace, and be less vulnerable to the damaging impact of bullies.

The Cool Factor

KIDS LISTEN AND TAKE TO HEART THE MESSAGES THEY RELATE TO AND they pass on the ones they think are cool. The Law helps students remember and communicate a profound message in an easy to understand metaphor and story. Their classmates, teammates, friends, neighbors, and family members all get the point. The Law of the Garbage Truck helps kids learn that it's not only right to stand up for someone, it's cool to stand up for someone.

Most teachers do not have time to implement another school program. Demands on teachers are significant enough. Teachers are not looking for complicated initiatives. They are in need of high-impact, easy to implement messages in the classroom. The Law of the Garbage Truck is one of those messages.

The Law of the Garbage Truck also complements character-building programs already in use at schools. For example, in 3,000 schools throughout the United States, Ron Wilber and other teachers use a program called Capturing Kids Hearts™. The program helps teachers "build positive, productive, trusting relationships—among themselves and with their students." The Safe School Ambassadors Program® is another program used in more than 550 schools.

Take Their Power Away

STUDENTS ALSO LEARN THAT BY FOLLOWING THE LAW OF THE GARBAGE Truck when they are the target of a bully, they can quickly diffuse the situation by just "smiling, waving, and wishing the bully well" and not taking it personally.

Psychologist Carl Pickhardt writes about how important it is not to take the teasing of others personally in his book *Why Good Kids Act Cruel*: "Words intended to wound cannot hurt without the victims choosing to take the mean words to heart. They take teasing to heart when they treat the taunts as truth. . . . Victims can remember how teasing always tells much more about the teaser than the teased—how it expresses a desire to be mean and usually attacks a trait about which the teaser feels threatened and insecure."

When we demonstrate to bullies that they lack the ability to hurt us, we take away their power.

Declare Your Zone

ONE OF THE EASIEST WAYS TO REINFORCE THE MESSAGE OF THE LAW OF THE Garbage Truck is to have students and teachers sign a No Garbage Trucks! Zone poster. The message is straightforward: "We don't accept garbage. We don't spread garbage. We are not Garbage Trucks!"

If you would like to download a free No Garbage Trucks! Zone poster for your school, visit www.thelawofthegarbagetruck.com. Let people know that you study, work, and play in a No Garbage Trucks! Zone.

Your Action Guide

We all connect to children in some way. We are parents, siblings, relatives, friends, neighbors, teachers, administrators, and community officials.

What can you do to enrich our schools for our children? How can you make sure that our schools are No Garbage Trucks! Zones?

Write below two ways you can help our children.

THE PLEDGE GLOBALLY

Forty-eight Languages, One Hundred Countries

Our true nationality is mankind.

—H.G. Wells

IN EVERY COUNTRY WHERE I HAVE HAD THE PRIVILEGE OF SHARING THE NO Garbage Trucks! Pledge, the impact has been the same: People's lives have been transformed.

Because I want people all over the world to experience the power of The No Garbage Trucks! Pledge, I've had it translated into almost fifty languages.

Arabic	Farsi	Japanese	Serbian
Armenian	Filipino	Kimeru	Shona
Azerbaijani	French	Latvian	Slovak
Bangla	Georgian	Macedonian	Spanish
Bavarian	German	Malay	Swahili
Bosnian	Greek	Maltese	Swedish
Bulgarian	Hebrew	Norwegian	Tagalog
Chinese	Hindi	Persian	Turkish
Czech	Hungarian	Polish	Twi
Danish	Icelandic	Portuguese	Ukrainian
Dutch	Indonesian	Romanian	Urdu
Estonian	Italian	Russian	Vietnamese

My goal is to have The No Garbage Trucks! Pledge translated into as many of the world's languages as possible. A current view of all the translations can be found at www.thelawofthegarbagetruck.com. If you would like to help me translate The No Garbage Trucks! Pledge into your language, let me know by sending an e-mail to: david@thelawofthegarbagetruck.com.

Reading Group Guidelines

Make your friends your teachers and mingle the pleasures of conversation with the advantages of instruction.

—Baltasar Gracián

I WONDER IF YOU DO THE SAME THING I DO. WHEN YOU DISCOVER something meaningful in your life—a new way of thinking, a strategy, or a philosophy—you tell all the important people in your life about it. You share what you have learned, and you ask what they think. You might even debate your new insight. If you do any of these things, you are not alone.

Learning Together

LEARNING IS RARELY AN INDIVIDUAL EXERCISE. WE LEARN BY SHARING.

Churches, temples, synagogues, and mosques host study groups. Businesses hold classes and meetings. Professional organizations run conferences. Friends organize book clubs, Bible study groups, and other get-togethers centered on common interests. Families share books, discuss ideas, and participate in activities together. And all of these efforts are what people have been doing with The Law of the Garbage Truck.

Business groups are talking about how to apply The Law and The Pledge to their customers, partners, teammates, and workplaces. Religious and spiritual groups are contemplating the lessons and discussing how they relate to scripture and sacred teachings. Group therapists are using the insights to help people reduce their anger and frustration and to help them focus on what is good in their lives. Holistic health groups are incorporating the lessons into their healing strategies, meditation classes, and exercise sessions.

Now, with *The Law of the Garbage Truck*, groups have an opportunity to take their learning even deeper. They can read and study this book together. They can fully explore what it means to live life in a No Garbage Trucks! Zone and help each other honor and fulfill The Eight No Garbage Trucks! Commitments.

Studying with David

I BELIEVE WE ALL HAVE A CALLING. MINE IS TO HELP PEOPLE LIVE MORE positive, engaged, and purposeful lives. This book helps me fulfill my mission. It allows me to connect with people wanting to live their best possible lives. For that reason, whenever possible, I have agreed to do book readings and give presentations by phone to interested reading groups.

If you would like me to speak to your reading group, e-mail me at david@thelawofthegarbagetruck.com.

Reading Group Guidelines

IF YOU ARE INTERESTED IN FORMING A GROUP TO STUDY *THE LAW OF THE Garbage Truck* or if you are already in a group, here are a number of ideas to help you get the most out of the experience.

Prior to the Meeting

1. Decide how many chapters or sections of *The Law of the Garbage Truck* you will discuss at each meeting. Some groups will take a chapter or two at a time, others a section. Some groups, particularly monthly book clubs, will read the book from cover to cover before their meeting and then discuss it in its entirety.

2. Choose someone to lead each meeting.

3. Ask group members to answer the Action Guide questions that follow each chapter.

4. Ask everyone to take the quizzes "Are You a Garbage Accepter?" and "Are You a Garbage Dumper?"

5. Set guidelines for the meeting. (A few of my suggestions follow.)

Beginning the Meeting

1. Group leaders summarize each chapter to be discussed. They review the key insights in each chapter.

2. Group leaders (or another member of the group) may also read aloud an entire story or a particular passage of a chapter before kicking off the discussion.

During the Meeting

1. Ask members to share their own personal experiences similar to the ones discussed in each chapter.

2. Ask members to share how they applied the insights in the chapters to their lives. Ask them what happened when they did. How did it help them?

3. Ask members to share their answers to each Action Guide question.

4. Ask members to share their insights after taking the quizzes "Are You a Garbage Accepter?" and "Are You a Garbage Dumper?" Ask them what they have been doing well. What was surprising? How can they improve?

5. Ask members to connect the lesson of each chapter to one of the sacred passages, biblical verses, or quotations at the beginning of each chapter. There is much to be learned by referring to the great works of religion, philosophy, history, psychology, and the arts.

6. Ask members to relate the message of the chapter in discussion to the values, standards, and missions of their organizations or businesses.

7. Ask members to discuss how they can create No Garbage Trucks! Zones in their lives, families, organizations, and companies.

General Guidelines

1. Seek to learn as much as you can from each other.

2. Encourage all members to share their ideas.

3. Have one person speak at a time.

4. Avoid side conversations whenever possible.

5. Agree to have spirited debates, but don't argue.

6. Set discussion time limits if needed.

7. Gently ensure that no one dominates the discussion.

8. Make sure the meetings are engaging and enjoyable.

9. Remember, improving our lives, not perfecting them, is the goal.

Other Study Groups

COUPLES, SIBLINGS, FRIENDS, AND TEAMMATES CAN ALSO DISCUSS HOW THIS book relates to their lives and share their answers to each Action Guide question. When people discover together how to achieve greater success and happiness in life, they open up new dimensions in their relationships and deepen their bonds.

The final and best advice for all of us when we study together is to follow the example of the ancient philosophers and religious scholars— fully engage our energy, attention, and commitment to our shared learning. By discussing, contemplating, and exploring everything, we get the most out of our experience with this book and with each other.

To learn more about *The Law of the Garbage Truck* reading groups, visit: www.thelawofthegarbagetruck.com.

Notes and References

Science is a way of thinking much more than it is a body of knowledge.
Its goal is to find out how the world works, to seek what regularities
there may be, to penetrate to the connections of things . . .

—Carl Sagan

Chapter One

ROY BAUMEISTER AND HIS COLLEAGUES ARGUE THAT BAD EVENTS HAVE A
more powerful impact on us than good ones (if we let them). See
Baumeister, R. F., E. Bratslavsky, C. Finkenauer, and K.D. Vohs. 2001. "Bad is
stronger than good." *Review of General Psychology* (vol. 5): 323–70.

Chapter Two

RICHARD LAZARUS AND SUSAN FOLKMAN DEMONSTRATE HOW THE HASSLES
of daily life can have a destructive impact on our happiness and health. See
Lazarus, R. S., and S. Folkman. *Stress, Appraisal, and Coping.* New York:
Springer, 1984.

ROBERT SAPOLSKY SHOWS HOW UNNECESSARY STRESS HAS A DAMAGING
effect in our lives. See Sapolsky, R. M. *Why Zebras Don't Get Ulcers.* New
York: Holt, 2004.

SONJA LYUBOMIRSKY OFFERS POWERFUL, SCIENCE-BASED ADVICE FOR
improving our happiness. See Lyubomirsky, S. *The How of Happiness.*
New York: Penguin, 2008.

Chapter Four

JULIA BOEHM AND SONJA LYUBOMIRSKY PRESENT A GROWING BODY OF evidence that shows how happy people are more likely to succeed in business. See Boehm, J. K., and S. Lyubomirsky. 2008. "Does happiness lead to career success?" *Journal of Career Assessment* (vol. 16): 101–16.

Chapter Five

THERE ARE FEW PEOPLE WHO BETTER EMBODY THE LAW OF THE GARBAGE Truck than Jackie Robinson. All quotations in this chapter were selected from Robinson's autobiography. See Robinson, J. *I Never Had It Made: An Autobiography of Jackie Robinson*. New York: HarperCollins, 1995.

Chapter Six

THE FINDINGS IN THIS PAPER ARE SO POWERFUL THAT I NEEDED TO reference it one more time. See Baumeister, R.F., E. Bratslavsky, C. Finkenauer, and K.D. Vohs. 2001. "Bad is stronger than good." *Review of General Psychology* (vol. 5): 323–70.

DANIEL GILBERT DEMONSTRATES IN HIS RESEARCH HOW OFTEN OUR MEMORY is faulty and our happiness predictions are wrong. See Gilbert, D. *Stumbling on Happiness*. New York: Knopf, 2006.

BRUCE PERRY REMINDS US IN THIS BOOK CHAPTER THAT, OUR BRAIN, MORE often than not, sends us false alarms; we do not need to fight or take cover every time we receive these messages. See Perry, B. D. "The Memories of States: How the Brain Stores and Retrieves Traumatic Experience." In *Splintered Reflections: Images of the Body in Trauma*, ed. J. M. Goodwin and R. Attias, 9–38. New York: Basic Books, 1999.

JONATHAN HAIDT CAUTIONS US THAT OUR SUBCONSCIOUS WILL RUN MORE of our lives than we would like if we are not mindful. In an early section of his book called "Mental Intrusions," Haidt references the compelling research of social psychologist Dan Wegner. See Haidt, J. *The Happiness Hypothesis: Finding Modern Truth in Ancient Wisdom*. New York: Basic Books, 2006.

Chapter Seven

KAREN REIVICH AND ANDREW SHATTE OFFER RESEARCH-BASED ADVICE on how to increase our resilience. See Reivich, K. and A. Shatte. *The Resilience Factor: 7 Keys to Finding Your Inner Strength and Overcoming Life's Hurdles*. New York: Broadway Books, 2003.

POSITIVE PSYCHOLOGY COFOUNDER MARTIN SELIGMAN MAKES IT CLEAR that pessimism is most often a burden, not a blessing. See Seligman, M.E.P. *Authentic Happiness: Using the New Positive Psychology to Realize Your Potential for Lasting Fulfillment*. New York: Free Press, 2002.

Chapter Eight

THE RARE DISEASE CEREBRAL LYMPHOMATOID GRANULOMATOSIS IS discussed in this research paper. See, Lucantoni, C., P. De Bonis, F. Doglietto, G. Esposito, L. Larocca, A. Mangiola, M. Martini, F. Papacci, L. Teofili, and A. Pompucci. 2009. "Primary cerebral lymphomatoid granulomatosis: report of four cases and literature review." *Journal of Neuro-Oncology*, 94 (no. 2): 235–42.

EDWARD HALLOWELL CLEARLY DISTINGUISHES BETWEEN HELPFUL WORRY and what he calls "toxic worry." See Hallowell, E. M. *Worry*. New York: Ballantine, 1998.

Chapter Nine

MARTIN SELIGMAN POINTS TO RESEARCH THAT SHOWS THAT VENTING our anger and frustration can be bad advice. See Seligman, M.E.P. *Authentic Happiness: Using the New Positive Psychology to Realize Your Potential for Lasting Fulfillment*. New York: Free Press, 2002.

TARA GALOVSKI AND EDWARD BLANCHARD DISCUSS THE MANY contributing factors that lead to road rage and the consequences of this dangerous behavior. See Galovski, T. E., and E. B. Blanchard. 2004. "Road Rage: A domain for psychological intervention." *Journal of Aggression and Violent Behavior* (vol. 9): 105–27.

BRAD BUSHMAN AND HIS COLLEAGUES CAUTION US THAT RUMINATING over negative events in our lives can lead us to take out our frustration on others. See Bushman, B., A. Bonacci, W. Pederson, E. Vasquez, and N. Miller. 2004. "Chewing on it can chew you up: Effects of rumination on triggered displaced aggression." *Journal of Personality and Social Psychology* (vol. 88, No. 6): 969–83.

Chapter Ten

FRED LUSKIN'S RESEARCH CONCLUDES THAT WE CAN INCREASE OUR happiness by forgiving others and ourselves. See Luskin, F. *Forgive for Love.* New York: HarperOne, 2009.

A LEADER IN THE FIELD OF FORGIVENESS RESEARCH, EVERETT WORTHINGTON presents his theories and research in this book. See Worthington, E. L. *Forgiveness and Reconciliation: Theory and Application.* New York: Routledge, 2006.

SONJA LYUBOMIRSKY OFFERS FURTHER EVIDENCE OF THE POWER OF forgiveness. See Lyubomirsky, S. *The How of Happiness.* New York: Penguin, 2008.

IN HIS BOOK, GEORGE VAILLANT SKILLFULLY BRINGS TOGETHER THE POWER of faith and science. See Vaillant, G. *Spiritual Evolution: A Scientific Defense of Faith.* New York: Broadway Books, 2008.

Chapter Eleven

BARBARA FREDRICKSON DEMONSTRATES HOW EXPERIENCING FREQUENT positive emotion is a crucial contributor to our happiness and success in life. See Fredrickson, B. L. *Positivity*. New York: Crown, 2009.

ONE OF THE LAST QUARTER-CENTURY'S MOST CELEBRATED CHIEF executives, Bill George, outlines what it takes to be a successful leader. See George, B. *Authentic Leadership*. San Francisco: Jossey-Bass, 2003.

Chapter Twelve

LOUIS FISCHER HAS IMPRESSIVELY COMPILED AND ORGANIZED GANDHI'S MOST powerful writings in this book. See Fischer, L. *The Essential Gandhi: An Anthology of His Writings on His Life, Work, and Ideas*. New York: Vintage, 1983.

STEPHEN POST'S RESEARCH CONVINCINGLY SHOWS HOW DOING GOOD makes us happier and healthier. See Neimark, J. and S. Post. *Why Good Things Happen to Good People: How to Live a Longer, Healthier, Happier Life by the Simple Act of Giving*. New York: Broadway Books, 2007.

Chapter Fourteen

THIS IS THE FIRST OF THREE REFERENCES TO NELSON MANDELA, A remarkable man and leader. See Mandela, N. *The Long Walk to Freedom: The Autobiography of Nelson Mandela*. New York: Back Bay Books, 1995.

Chapter Eighteen

DEBORAH RUPP AND SHARMIN SPENCER SHOW HOW "CUSTOMER interactional injustice" leads to increased "emotional labor" in customer service representatives, clearly demonstrating the need to help customer service representatives respond more effectively to difficult customers. See Rupp, D. E. and S. Spencer. 2006. "When customers lash out: The effects of customer interactional injustice on emotional labor and the mediating role of discrete emotions." *Journal of Applied Psychology* (vol. 91, No. 4): 971–78.

Chapter Nineteen

SHELLY GABLE AND HER RESEARCH COLLEAGUES SHOW HOW CRITICAL IT IS for us to be highly and positively engaged when the people we care about share their good news with us. See Gable, S. L., H. T. Reis, E. A. Impett, and E. R. Asher. 2004. "What do you do when things go right? The intrapersonal and interpersonal benefits of sharing positive events." *Journal of Personality and Social Psychology* (87, No. 2): 228–45.

Chapter Twenty

EVERETT WORTHINGTON'S RESEARCH CONFIRMS THE HEALING POWER OF forgiveness. See Worthington, E. L. *Forgiveness and Reconciliation: Theory and Application.* New York: Routledge, 2006.

Chapter Twenty-two

IN THEIR BOOK ON HAPPINESS, ED DIENER AND ROBERT BISWAS-DIENER bring to life over thirty years of cutting-edge research on how to achieve real psychological wealth. See Diener, E. and R. Biswas-Diener. *Happiness: Unlocking the Mysteries of Psychological Wealth.* New York: Wiley-Blackwell, 2008.

Chapter Twenty-three

RICHARD LAZARUS AND SUSAN FOLKMAN SHOW US HOW OUR COMMITMENTS underpin our actions in life. See Lazarus, R. S. and S. Folkman. *Stress, Appraisal, and Coping.* New York: Springer, 1984.

ROBERT SAPOLSKY PRESENTS COMPELLING EVIDENCE THAT OVERREACTING to provocations can have a disastrous impact on our health. See Sapolsky, R. M. *Why Zebras Don't Get Ulcers.* New York: Holt, 2004.

THE BIBLICAL PASSAGES CITED IN THIS BOOK ARE TAKEN FROM THE NEW International Version® Bible or the New King James Version® Bible. The only exception is my reference to Ecclesiastes 5:5. In this instance, I prefer the original King James translation for its poetry.

Chapter Twenty-four

JOHN GOTTMAN'S RESEARCH FORMS THE BASIS FOR THIS PRACTICAL GUIDE to improving our marriages. See DeClaire, J. and J. Gottman. *The Relationship Cure: A Five-Step Guide to Strengthening Your Marriage, Family, and Friendships.* New York: Three Rivers Press, 2001.

ROY BAUMEISTER AND HIS COLLEAGUES PRESENT GROUND-BREAKING research that shows we have a limited capacity to exhibit self-control. See Baumeister, R. F., K. Vohs, and D. Tice. 2007. "The strength model of self control." *Current Directions in Psychological Science* (vol. 16, no. 6): 351–55.

ROY BAUMEISTER PRESENTS RESEARCH THAT DEMONSTRATES INCREASING our self-control has positive outcomes in our lives. See Baumeister, R. F. 2002. "Ego depletion and self-control failure: An energy model of the self's executive function." *Self and Identity* (vol. 1): 129–36.

Chapter Twenty-five

THIS BOOK INTRODUCES JOHN GOTTMAN'S 5:1 POSITIVITY RATIO AS A powerful predictor of successful marriages. See Gottman, J. *Why Marriages Succeed or Fail . . . And How You Can Make Yours Last.* New York: Simon & Schuster, 1994.

Chapter Twenty-six

ELIZABETH KÜBLER-ROSS AND DAVID KESSLER OFFER A COMFORTING BOOK for people who are grieving. See Kübler-Ross, E. and D. Kessler. *On Grief and Grieving: Finding the Meaning of Grief Through the Five Stages of Loss.* New York: Scribner, 2007.

Chapter Twenty-seven

THROUGH HIS GROUND-BREAKING RESEARCH, GEORGE BONANNO HELPS people see how happiness is again possible after suffering loss. See

Bonanno, G. *The Spiritual Side of Sadness: What the New Science of Bereavement Tells Us About Life After Loss*. New York: Basic Books, 2009.

Chapter Twenty-eight

DANIEL SIEGEL MAKES IT CLEAR HOW IMPORTANT IT IS THAT WE INCREASE our mindfulness in life. See Siegel, D. J. *The Mindful Brain: Reflection and Attunement in the Cultivation of Well-Being*. New York: Norton, 2007.

Chapter Twenty-nine

AFTER CONDUCTING AN EXTENSIVE REVIEW OF WELL-BEING LITERATURE AND research, and testing two happiness-increasing interventions, Sonja Lyubomirsky, Ken Sheldon, and David Schkade demonstrate in their paper that change is possible. See Lyubomirsky, S., K. M. Sheldon, and D. Schkade. 2005. "Pursuing happiness: the architecture of sustainable change." *Review of General Psychology* (vol. 9): 111–31.

SONJA LYUBOMIRSKY EXPLAINS "THE SUSTAINABLE HAPPINESS MODEL" SHE developed with Ken Sheldon and David Schkade. See Lyubomirsky, S. *The How of Happiness*. New York: Penguin, 2008.

Chapter Thirty

ELAINE HATFIELD, JOHN CACIOPPO, AND RICHARD RAPSON PROVIDE compelling evidence of how we "catch" other people's emotions and how we spread ours. See Hatfield, E., J. T. Cacioppo, and R. L. Rapson. *Emotional Contagion*. Cambridge: Cambridge University Press, 1994.

NICHOLAS CHRISTAKIS AND JAMES FOWLER MAKE IT CLEAR HOW OUR behavior has a far-reaching influence on others. See Christakis, N. A. and J. H. Fowler. *Connected: The Surprising Power of Our Social Networks and How They Shape Our Lives*. New York: Little, Brown, 2009.

CHRISTINE PEARSON AND CHRISTINE PORATH LAY OUT A POWERFUL argument for increasing civility at work. See Pearson, C. and C. Porath. *The Cost of Bad Behavior: How Incivility Is Damaging Your Business and What to Do About It.* New York: Portfolio, 2009.

CHRISTINE PEARSON, LYNNE ANDERSSON, AND CHRISTINE PORATH HAVE been researching the destructive effects of incivility in the workplace for more than a decade. See Pearson, C., L. Andersson, and C. Porath. 2000. "Assessing and attacking workplace incivility." *Organizational Dynamics* (vol. 29, no. 2): 123–37.

KIM CAMERON PERSUASIVELY DEMONSTRATES HOW IMPORTANT THE findings of the emerging field of positive organizational scholarship are to the successful running of a business. See Cameron, K. *Positive Leadership: Strategies for Extraordinary Performance.* San Francisco: Berrett-Koehler, 2008.

Chapter Thirty-one

NELSON MANDELA'S AUTOBIOGRAPHY OPENS A WINDOW INTO THE LIFE OF one of the world's great leaders. See Mandela, N. *The Long Walk to Freedom: The Autobiography of Nelson Mandela.* New York: Back Bay Books, 1995.

STEPHEN CARTER MAKES ONE OF THE MOST PERSUASIVE ARGUMENTS for the importance of civility in our lives. See Carter, S. *Civility: Manners, Morals, and the Etiquette of Democracy.* New York: Basic Books, 1998.

GARY AND RUTH NAMIE SHOW THE DESTRUCTIVE IMPACT BULLIES HAVE AT work. See Namie, G. and R. Namie. *The Bully at Work: What You Can Do to Stop the Hurt and Reclaim Your Dignity on the Job.* Naperville: Sourcebooks, 2009.

CHRISTOPHER PETERSON DISCUSSES THE IMPORTANCE OF LIVING IN accordance with your values and developing good character. See Peterson, C. *A Primer in Positive Psychology.* New York: Oxford University Press, 2006.

Chapter Thirty-two

BARBARA FREDRICKSON AND MARCIAL LOSADA DEMONSTRATE THE importance of cultivating and sustaining positive emotions in business. See Fredrickson, B. L. and M. F. Losada. 2005. "Positive affect and the complex dynamics of human flourishing." *American Psychologist* (vol. 60): 678–86.

THE UNITED STATES VETERANS HEALTH ADMINISTRATION CARES FOR millions of veterans and their families each year. See *www.va.gov.*

Chapter Thirty-four

"STANFORD PRISON EXPERIMENT" CREATOR PHILIP ZIMBARDO KNOWS BETTER than most researchers what leads good people to do bad things. See Zimbardo, P. *The Lucifer Effect: Understanding How Good People Turn Evil.* New York: Random House, 2007.

NELSON MANDELA'S EXAMPLE INSPIRES US TO FOCUS ON WHAT'S important in life. See Mandela, N. *The Long Walk to Freedom: The Autobiography of Nelson Mandela.* New York: Back Bay Books, 1995.

Appendix: A Special No Garbage Trucks! Zone—Our Schools

RICK PHILLIPS, JOHN LINNEY, AND CHRIS PACK MAKE A RESEARCH-BASED case that bullying is rampant in our schools, and nurturing student leaders is a powerful way of turning the tide in the bullying epidemic. See Linney, M., C. Pack, and R. Phillips. *Safe School Ambassadors: Harnessing Student Power to Stop Bullying and Violence.* San Francisco: Jossey-Bass, 2008.

BASED ON THEIR EXTENSIVE RESEARCH, DEBRA PEPLER AND WENDY CRAIG outline what we can do to reduce bullying behavior in schools. See Pepler, D. and W. Craig. 2000. "Making a difference in bullying." *LaMarsh Centre for Research and Conflict Resolution,* York University (rep. 60): 1–37.

WENDY CRAIG AND DEBRA PEPLER DEMONSTRATE HOW PREVALENT BULLYING is in our schools and how peers are involved in a majority of bullying incidents. See Craig, W. and D. Pepler. 1997. "Observations of bullying and victimization in the school yard." *Canadian Journal of School Psychology* (vol. 13, no. 2): 41–60.

THROUGH THEIR CAPTURING KIDS HEARTS™ PROGRAM, THE FLIPPEN GROUP has helped thousands of teachers provide a more enriching environment for their students. See *http://www.flippengroup.com/education/ckh.html.*

CARL PICKHARDT OFFERS A THOUGHTFUL AND PRACTICAL GUIDE FOR escaping the claws of bullying. See Pickhardt, C. *Why Good Kids Act Cruel: The Hidden Truth about the Pre-Teen Years.* Naperville: Sourcebooks, 2010.

Thank You, Taxi Drivers

Let us be grateful to people who make us happy; they
are the charming gardeners who make our souls blossom.

—Marcel Proust

WHEN I WAS GROWING UP, MY FATHER TAUGHT ME TO APPRECIATE AND respect taxi drivers. He said they were great drivers and that their minds were like global positioning satellites: They knew every destination and the best way to get there.

My father also taught me that taxi drivers know a lot about people, as they have seen most of us in just about every life circumstance. Taxi drivers witness the good and not so good things we do. They're interesting, and we can learn a lot from them.

Each time I jump into a taxi, I strike up a conversation with the driver. When I travel with a group of people and one of us has to sit up front, I volunteer. When I talk with a taxi driver, I learn something new every time.

So I want to thank everyone who drives a cab. Thank you for driving me wherever I have needed to go. Thank you for being there in all types of weather, day and night. Thank you for the wisdom you have shared with me over the years.

Special thanks to a taxi driver who once smiled and waved at a Garbage Truck.

Thank You, Real Garbage Collectors

The first wealth is health.

—Ralph Waldo Emerson

THIS BOOK WOULD NOT BE COMPLETE WITHOUT THANKING THE MEN AND women who drive the real garbage trucks in our communities. Garbage collectors pick up and dispose of our refuse so that we can live in a healthy, clean environment.

The job of a garbage collector is not easy. We give them garbage that's heavy, hard to handle, and difficult to transport. We ask them to dispose of it as far away from us as possible. And we make their jobs even more complicated when we walk and drive all around them as they make their daily rounds.

Given the challenging nature of their job, real garbage collectors know the importance of following The Law of the Garbage Truck.

I am grateful to these men and women who help keep our world beautiful.

Acknowledgments

I learned long ago that everything good in my life has come as a result of the help from family, friends, teammates, colleagues, and strangers. Someone, somewhere is always helping me with something. My work is never accomplished alone. This book is the most recent example of how I have been blessed in my life. I have many people to thank, including you.

I will forever be grateful to my parents, who have given me so much.

Mom has played a uniquely important role in my writing. When I began as a newspaper columnist, I asked Mom to proofread my articles. Thousands of words later, Mom has edited every column I have published. She was also my preliminary editor for this book. Mom is an amazing woman, joyful in her presence, wise in her counsel, and abundant in her love.

Throughout my life, I have leaned on the strength, support, and humor of my dad. Dad will do anything to help my business, and he does the same thing—as does Mom—for my family. He's also a human billboard for The Law of the Garbage Truck; Dad doesn't leave the house unless he's wearing one of our shirts or hats.

The best days of my life began the day I met my wife, Dawn. Her love sustains me. No one can make me laugh the way she can. Dawn believes in everything I do and appreciates me to the core. She has supported me in every way during the writing of this book, including reviewing numerous drafts along the way.

Life with Dawn became even more beautiful when Eliana was born in 2002, and again when Ariela was born in 2003. Eliana and Ariela bring so much joy to our lives. My girls have been little cheerleaders for the book, and they know The Pledge by heart.

I am thankful to my brother Mike, for his love and belief in me. I am also grateful to Mike's wife, Halle; Dawn's parents, Terry and Marcia Gano; and Dawn's brother, Nate. I want to thank all my friends, clients, and colleagues for their support, especially Robert and Susan Aliota, Alberto and Laura Casellas, and Preston and Cari Lewis.

When I finished *The Law of the Garbage Truck*, it was my friend and colleague in positive psychology, Caroline Miller, who said, "You have to get this book published immediately." (Thanks, Caroline.) I listened to her. She introduced me to her agent, Ivor Whitson. A former president of two publishing firms, Ivor became my agent. He's an incredible agent and one of the nicest men I have ever known. His knowledge and guidance through the publishing process have been invaluable. Then came Jennifer Williams, my editor at Sterling Publishing. Jennifer believed in *The Law of the Garbage Truck* from the beginning. Her support, encouragement, and brilliant editing have been critical to the success of this project. This book also couldn't have happened without the vision of editorial vice president Michael Fragnito. Michael saw the impact this book could have globally, and championed the book at every opportunity. I'm also grateful to Marcus Leaver, president of Sterling, for his personal support of the project. I'm thankful to other key members of the Sterling Team who have supported and promoted the book from the beginning, including Jason Prince, Leigh Ann Ambrosi, Karen Patterson, Josh Wood, Caroline Mann, Megan Perritt, Megan Murphy, Leah Eagel, Marilyn Kretzer, Sandra Ribicic, Emma Gonzales, Sasha Tropp, Mary Hern, Barbara Noe, Rebecca Maines, Elizabeth Mihaltse, Christine Heun, and Bob Steimle.

I want to thank Chris Abbott for his good work at The Momentum Project. Chris reviewed numerous drafts of this book and his feedback was tremendously valuable.

Thanks also to Stephanie Gunning for helping me make sure my book was ready to share with publishers. Stephanie's insights, questions, and editing were invaluable. Brenda Robinson also provided timely and sharp copyediting support.

Thanks to everyone who reviewed and provided important input to all or parts of my book: Katie Bassler, Kaitlin Keegan, Brenda Richterkessing, Roger Kumar, Frank Mosca, Robert Aliota, Susan Aliota, Dawn Pollay, David Schmidt, Becky Remmel, Joan Grossman, Kirk Froggatt, Tamara Cooper, Ronnie Whitson, Cari Lewis, Preston Kevin Lewis, Laura Casellas, Alberto Casellas, Halle Pollay, Mike Pollay, Margaret Greenberg, and Skip Wise. Thanks also to everyone who shared their stories with me: Barbara

Saltzman, Susan Aliota, Kim Greenbaum, Mihir Gosalia, Athan Ray, Karyn Hoffmann, Tanna Tuttle, Nathan Gano, Tamara Cooper, Ron Wilber, Hope Shasha, Laura Casellas, Suzie and James Kahlil, and Eric Lochtefeld.

Thank you also to all the students in Ron Wilber's classes who wrote about the impact of The Law in their lives, particularly Alec, Jacqueline, and Stephanie.

Thanks also to Katie Otis for her website support and graphic design work, including the cover of this book; Christine Benjamin for her illustrations; Todd Remmel for his early website support; Chelsea Seely for typing large portions of my manuscript.

I want to thank all the leaders who have declared that their organizations are No Garbage Trucks! Zones. I particularly want to thank JoAnne Renz, Linda Belton, and Magdalena Veigl of the Veteran's Health Administration; Juan Cajiao of AIESEC; Preston Kevin Lewis of Warner Bros. Consumer Products; Carolyn Gable of New Age Transportation; Robert Aliota of Carolina Seal; Ron Wilber of Western Pines Middle School; Tammy Ferguson and Rudy Collum of The Village Academy; Randy Rose of The Main Place; Jayne Kupperman of The Education Network; Lenora Johnson of Steel Magnolias Breast Cancer Support Group; and Rev. Linda Mobley of Cason United Methodist Church.

Thank you to all the editors and publishers of the newspapers and news websites that publish and distribute my writing in print and online. John Johnston, former editor of *The Boca Raton News*, and Anita Finley, publisher of *Boomer Times* and Senior *Life Magazine*, were the first to print my columns "The Law of the Garbage Truck" and "Beware of Garbage Trucks!". Dan and Angie Calabrese, owners of North Star Writers Group, the syndication company that distributed my weekly column, have been great supporters. Thanks also to Senia Maymin, publisher of Positive Psychology News Daily. I'm also grateful to the team at HappyNews.com, especially editor Emily Johnson and publisher Byron Reese.

Thanks to Steve Siebold for his early input on the way I present The Law of the Garbage Truck story in my speeches and seminars. Thanks to Nick Morgan and Nikki Smith-Morgan for helping me communicate the depth of this book in my keynote speeches. Thanks to John Spannuth,

Ed Lamont, Dawn Siebold, Dorothy Lynn, Rosie Feeley, Cindy Rold, and Doug Hanson for their support. I'm also grateful to Nido Qubein, Ramsey Qubein, and Vicki Motsinger for their support. Thanks also to Tom Rath and Rick Brandon for offering timely encouragement when I was just beginning to write this book.

I want to thank everyone who helped bring The Law of the Garbage Truck to television: Joan Grossman, David Schmidt, Becky Remmel, Steve Greenbaum, and Anthony Salerno. Special thanks to David Schmidt and Becky Remmel for bringing their passion and belief in The Law of the Garbage Truck to our road tour. Thanks also to David Yellen for my author photographs, and Gail Chatelain for the photos of me on top of a garbage truck.

I want to thank everyone who has played an important role in my work in positive psychology. I am particularly grateful to James Pawelski, Debbie Swick, Karen Reivich, Martin Seligman, Chris Peterson, Ed Diener, Sonja Lyubomirsky, Bill Robertson, Barbara Fredrickson, and Ray Fowler for their support during graduate school at the University of Pennsylvania and over the past few years. I'm also grateful to my colleagues in the International Positive Psychology Association for their encouragement.

Thank you to AIESEC, the world's largest student-run leadership development program. Leaders at all levels in AIESEC have taken The No Garbage Trucks! Pledge and have been spreading the message of The Law of the Garbage Truck to people internationally.

I also want to thank all the AIESEC leaders around the globe who have helped translate The No Garbage Trucks! Pledge into nearly fifty languages.

Finally, I want to thank *you* again.

When we embrace the special forces at work in our lives, we realize we are never alone and that we are always supported.

You are one of those special forces in my life.

Thank you for reading this book.

Thank you for making the world a more beautiful place.

Resources

YOUR JOURNEY DOES NOT HAVE TO END HERE. WHEN SOMETHING WORKS, you keep going. You do more of it. You build on what you've begun.

The following are resources to help you keep your momentum. You can find them all by visiting:

www.thelawofthegarbagetruck.com.

The Law of the Garbage Truck DVD

THE LAW OF THE GARBAGE TRUCK DVD IS FOR PEOPLE WHO WANT TO experience the visual power of David's message. In his DVD, David reenacts The Law of the Garbage Truck. The program was shot in Times Square and other locations in New York City. Also included is David's No Garbage Trucks! Pledge. David has people on the streets of New York City take The Pledge, as well as audiences from around the world. You'll also see The Pledge taken in multiple languages.

In 2009, The Law of the Garbage Truck was honored with The Award of Excellence, the top prize offered by the prestigious Annual Communicator Awards. The Communicator Awards are sanctioned and judged by the International Academy of the Visual Arts, an invitation-only body of top-tier executives from organizations such as Brandweek, Coach, Disney, Estee Lauder, HBO, Monster.com, MTV, Polo Ralph Lauren, Wired, and Yahoo!.

The Audio Book

DAVID RECORDED *THE LAW OF THE GARBAGE TRUCK* IN ITS ENTIRETY. HIS recording is available on CDs and as an audio download.

Speaking

DAVID SHARES THE LAW OF THE GARBAGE TRUCK WITH LIVE AUDIENCES throughout the United States and around the world. He leads them through the powerful and liberating group process of taking The No Garbage Trucks! Pledge together. If you are interested in rapidly transforming your organization into a No Garbage Trucks! Zone, invite David to one of your events.

Licensing

YOU CAN LICENSE THE LAW OF THE GARBAGE TRUCK™ PROGRAM FOR USE in your organization. Visit our website for more information.

Products

REINFORCE THE LAW OF THE GARBAGE TRUCK MESSAGE IN YOUR LIFE WITH fun and meaningful items for your home and workplace. Visit our website for a full selection of available products.

Newsletter

IN ORDER TO REMAIN CONNECTED TO THE LAW OF THE GARBAGE TRUCK mission, sign up for David's free newsletter. You'll join a network of people from more than 100 countries. You'll receive the latest resources and updates from The Law of the Garbage Truck. David will also share strategies to help you "Enjoy every day. Do what you love. Make a difference.™"

Blog and Social Networking Sites

STAY CONNECTED TO THE MOST UP TO DATE NEWS ABOUT THE LAW OF THE Garbage Truck, interact with like-minded people, receive access to valuable resources, and keep up with David's latest projects (and how you can participate in them) by joining him on Facebook, My Space, LinkedIn, Twitter, and other social and business networking sites.

To follow David's blog, go to: www.pollayblog.com

Free Downloads

VISIT OUR WEBSITE FOR MORE RESOURCES THAT WILL HELP YOU LIVE YOUR life in a No Garbage Trucks!™ Zone.

Print The No Garbage Trucks! Pledge.

Print a No Garbage Trucks! Zone poster.

Print The Eight No Garbage Trucks! Commitments.

Print The Garbage Truck Communication Rule.

Print *The Law of the Garbage Truck* Reading Group Guidelines.

Invite a family member, friend, or co-worker to learn The Law of the Garbage Truck and take The No Garbage Trucks! Pledge.

Watch The No Garbage Trucks! Pledge.

The Law of the Garbage Truck Awards

AFTER DAVID LEARNED ABOUT THE IMPORTANT WORK OF STEEL MAGNOLIAS (highlighted earlier in the book), our organization recognized Steel Magnolias Breast Cancer Support Group, Inc. with "The Law of the Garbage Truck Award." We honored Steel Magnolias for the work they are doing to bring about a better world.

If you know of organizations or individuals doing good work in the world, you can nominate them to receive The Law of the Garbage Truck Award.

To learn more about the award, and all of the resources described above, visit:

www.thelawofthegarbagetruck.com.

Index

About the Author

DAVID J. POLLAY, M.A.P.P., IS ON A MISSION TO INCREASE HAPPINESS, SUCCESS, and civility in life and business. David's The Law of the Garbage Truck is an international phenomenon that's revolutionizing the way people relate to each other. "The Law" has been endorsed by psychologists, educators, professional athletes, entertainers, and business and spiritual leaders. Translated into forty-eight languages, David's No Garbage Trucks! Pledge has been taken by people from more than one hundred countries.

He is an internationally sought-after speaker and seminar leader whose work has been featured on NPR, Sirius Satellite Radio, ABC television, Univision, and in *Crain's New York Business*, *BusinessWeek Small Biz* magazine, and newspapers around the world. He is a founding associate executive director of the International Positive Psychology Association, and a visiting scholar at the University of Pennsylvania.

David's syndicated column is published in newspapers, magazines, newsletters, and online news sites worldwide. He also writes a popular blog, PollayBlog.com

He is president of The Momentum Project, LLC, a consulting organization focused on applying The Law of the Garbage Truck and the science of positive psychology to becoming happier and more successful in business and life. He has held leadership positions at Yahoo!, MasterCard, Global Payments, and AIESEC.

David holds a master's degree of applied positive psychology (M.A.P.P.) from the University of Pennsylvania, and a bachelor's degree in economics from Yale University. He lives in Florida with his wife and their two daughters.

Your No Garbage Trucks!
Pledge Cards

If wisdom were offered me with the proviso that I should keep
it shut up and refrain from declaring it, I should refuse.
There's no delight in owning anything unshared.

—Lucius Annaeus Seneca

WHEN I FIRST WROTE THE NO GARBAGE TRUCKS PLEDGE, I MEMORIZED IT. I PUT
a copy in my wallet. I wanted it with me. I had made a commitment. I would
not accept garbage. I would not dump garbage. I was not a Garbage Truck!

Now, I want you to have your own No Garbage Trucks! Pledge card.
There are four on the next page, and one of them is for you. I want you to
carry it with you wherever you go. Your card will remind you to let Garbage
Trucks pass you by, and to stop dumping garbage on others.

The other three cards are for your family, friends, or coworkers who
struggle with Garbage Trucks. Offer your support. Tell them about The Law
of the Garbage Truck. Then, give them a No Garbage Trucks! Pledge card.
It may be just what they're looking for.

When we help each other honor our No Garbage Trucks! Pledge,
we improve our relationships, strengthen our businesses, and bring
our communities together. Our goal is not perfection, just increased
happiness, success, and civility for everyone.

Feel good knowing that every time you let a Garbage Truck pass you
by, and each time you stop yourself from dumping on others, you make the
world a better place.

—DAVID J. POLLAY

www.TheLawoftheGarbageTruck.com

Visit our website to get involved in our latest projects, attend our
seminars, and receive our blog posts, tweets, and newsletters. You'll find
exercises, polls, quizzes, articles, reading group guidelines, podcasts, and
videos. We're looking forward to seeing you there!